Wholesome
Sugarfree
COOKING

Ray and Malinda Yutzy
RR 1 Box 118 A
Princeton, MO 64673

First Printing March 2005, 7.5M
Second Printing January 2006, 7.5M
Third Printing November 2006, 7.5M
Fourth Printing June 2007, 10M
Fifth Printing July 2008, 10M
Sixth Printing September 2009, 10M

2673 TR 421
Sugarcreek, OH 44681

Carlisle Printing
OF WALNUT CREEK Ltd.

Table of Contents

Foreword

We are living in a land of plenty. Food is to be had in abundance. Medicines and supplements can be obtained with ease. Millions of dollars have been spent in developing high-tech methods of sanitary food processing. Many more millions have been spent in medical research.

Why then are so many of us weak and sickly? Why do we have rapidly escalating rates of death from diseases that were practically unknown as little as one hundred years ago? Is it possible that some of the popular *advancements* in food and medicine are not to our benefit? Perhaps some of these drugstore pills and highly processed foods are not what God designed for the maintenance of our bodies. What are we doing or eating differently than what our ancestors did?

There are many conflicting theories as to what we should eat for better health. Like most other people, we too have indulged in the highly processed and refined foods from our local supermarket.

As we became more concerned about our family's health we learned about the low-fat and high-carb plan. Realizing that this was not working we began searching for alternatives. We learned of many different diets, from vegetarian to the Atkins, Pritiken, Zone, raw food, blood type, and numerous others. All of these diets claimed to be the answer to today's health problems.

Trying to choose the right way to eat from all the popular "health" diets became very frustrating and often overwhelming. Many times we became discouraged and wondered if it was really worth it. Finally we found a body of research that cut right through the confusion of all these different approaches. The basis of this research is in the study of the dietary habits of healthy people throughout history.

As recently as the 1930s, Dr. Weston Price traveled worldwide studying isolated people in many different countries. He found a similar pattern in practically all these different cultures. Although their diets varied considerably, as long as they ate their traditional, whole, unrefined foods, they enjoyed superb health and sound teeth. Soon after adapting to a diet of sugared, processed, and devitalized modern foods they became weak and sickly, plagued with rotten teeth and many diseases of modern man.

Before 1910 cancer and heart disease were very rare. Today they cause an estimated 70% of all deaths in the U.S. Almost 50% of all Americans battle with chronic illnesses.

In conclusion: Healthy people ate simple wholesome foods throughout history. We believe these traditional foods can still nourish us back to health even today.

Throughout this cookbook you will find health-related articles on a variety of foods we buy and use. To summarize these articles: The more closely we can get our food products to how God made them, the better they are for our bodies. We have also included some verses of Scripture to show an example of what God's chosen people ate in Biblical times.

We sincerely hope that this book will help you make the right choices in selecting wholesome foods for you and your families.

—*Raymond & Malinda Yutzy*

Thank You

We would like to give a big thank-you to everyone that took the time and effort to send recipes. Without your help this book would not be in existence. Thank you to all who wrote a note or letter along with your recipes. They were interesting and encouraging, and it makes us wish to meet you all personally. Also a thank-you to our moms, sisters, nieces, and nephew for help in copying recipes; to our children for going on with our work while we were busy with this project.

—*Raymond & Malinda Yutzy*

Introduction

It is our wish that this book will help people who are cooking and eating the natural way, and that it will encourage people who have health problems or want to stay healthy to also eat naturally.

If you want to change your way of eating, go slowly, so your taste buds will have a chance to adjust. Most people are used to having the sweet taste in about everything they eat. Try using less sugar and start using honey. Once your taste buds get used to not just tasting sweet, they can appreciate other flavors more. When converting a recipe asking for 1 c. sugar, use ½ c. honey; 1 c. white flour, use ¾ c. wheat flour; 1 c. shortening or margarine, use ¾ c. butter and ¼ c. oil.

If at all possible, buy your own wheat berries, etc. and grind your own flour. It is far superior as far as taste and texture to store-bought whole grain flours.

Use more spices and seasonings when cooking and baking.

As you will notice, in this book we used recipes asking for ingredients such as cream of mushroom soup, taco seasoning, corn chips, cream cheese, etc. You can find recipes for making these ingredients in here also. As all cooks know, a lot of our time is spent in the kitchen and a lot more so if we make our own instead of using store-bought and packaged foods. But it eases one's mind to know that we can make our own and know what is in it.

Use the health hints and remedies as you see fit. Quite a few of them we know work, and we use them as the need arises.

—*Raymond & Malinda Yutzy*

Breakfast

Oatmeal Waffles

2 eggs, beaten
2 c. buttermilk
1 c. quick-cooking oats
1 Tbsp. molasses
1 Tbsp. oil
1 c. whole wheat flour

½ tsp. salt
1 tsp. soda
1 tsp. baking powder

In a large bowl, mix eggs and buttermilk. Add oats and mix well. Stir in molasses and oil. Combine flour, salt, soda, and baking powder. Stir into the egg mixture. If batter is too thick, thin with a little milk. This recipe works well for pancakes as well.

Note: If buttermilk is not available, a good substitute is to mix well: 1 c. sweet milk and 1 c. plain yogurt. Or use 2 c. sour milk.

—*Mrs. Joe Garber, Prattsburgh, NY*

Oatmeal Pancakes

2 c. buttermilk
1½ c. quick oats
2 eggs, separated
⅓ c. butter
1 Tbsp. honey

1 tsp. salt
1 tsp. soda
1 tsp. baking powder
1 c. whole wheat flour

Pour buttermilk over oats and let stand for five minutes. Beat egg yolks. Add butter, honey, soaked oats, then dry ingredients. Fold in beaten egg whites. Drop by tablespoonful onto a hot griddle to fry.

—*Mrs. Raymond Fisher, Rebersburg, PA*

Happiness is doing with a smile what you have to do anyway.

Whole Wheat Pancakes

2 c. whole wheat flour	2 eggs, beaten
1 tsp. soda	1¾ c. milk
2 tsp. baking powder	¼ c. olive oil
½ tsp. salt	¼ c. vinegar
2 Tbsp. honey	

Add ingredients in order given. Don't beat too much. For waffles or fluffy pancakes, beat egg whites separately and add last.

—*Lydia Fisher, Jersey Shore, PA*

Potato Pancakes

3 c. finely shredded, peeled potatoes, well drained
2 eggs, beaten   ½ tsp. salt
1½ Tbsp. whole wheat flour   ½ tsp. grated onion
⅛ tsp. baking powder

Mix together potatoes and eggs. In a mixing bowl, gently combine dry ingredients and onion. Stir into potatoes. Drop by tablespoonsful onto hot greased skillet. Brown slightly on both sides. Serve with applesauce or maple syrup.

—*Amelia Troyer, Glenford, OH*

Follow peace with all men, and holiness, without which no man shall see the Lord. Looking diligently lest any man fail of the grace of God; lest any root of bitterness springing up trouble you, and thereby many be defiled.

—Hebrews 12:14-15

Honey-Apple Pancakes

1¼ c. flour	1½ Tbsp. oil
¼ tsp. salt	1 tsp. baking powder
2 tsp. baking powder	¾ c. apple juice
⅛ tsp. apple pie spice	2 Tbsp. honey
⅛ tsp. baking soda	1 Tbsp. oil
¼ tsp. cinnamon	1 apple, finely chopped
1½ Tbsp. water	

In medium bowl stir together flour, salt, 2 tsp. baking powder, apple pie spice, soda, and cinnamon. Mix water, 1½ Tbsp. oil, and, 1 tsp. baking powder together. In a small bowl, add the other wet ingredients and chopped apple; add all at once to flour, stirring until blended, but still slightly lumpy. Let batter rest 2-3 minutes. Fry in hot oil.

—Laura Yoder, Free Union, VA

Cornmeal Pancakes

1 c. cornmeal	4 Tbsp. olive oil
1 c. whole grain flour	2 eggs, beaten
6 tsp. baking powder, rounded	⅛ tsp. stevia
1 tsp. Real salt	1 c. milk or buttermilk

Mix all together in order given. Fry in hot oil. Eat with pure maple syrup.

—Mrs. Daniel V. Gingerich, Woodsfield, OH

But seek ye first the kingdom of God, and His righteousness;
and all these things shall be added unto you.
—Matthew 6:33

French Toast, Oven Baked

2 eggs, beaten	½ tsp. vanilla
½ c. milk	6 slices whole wheat bread
½ tsp. salt	

Combine first four ingredients. Dip bread slices in egg mixture. Place on well-greased cookie sheet that has been generously sprinkled with dry bread crumbs. Sprinkle more bread crumbs on top, then drizzle with melted butter. Bake at 450° for 10 minutes, turning once during baking. Serve with syrup or sauce.

—Joanna Frantz, Camden, IN

Müesli

2 c. wheat germ	2 apples, grated
2 c. oatmeal	3 bananas, sliced
1 c. ground pecans	2 c. fresh pineapple slivers
2 c. coconut	or other canned fruit
32 oz. plain yogurt	milk to moisten if needed

Stir everything together till evenly moistened. Serve with a little maple syrup drizzled over top.

—Mrs. Naomi Ruth Bontrager, Mio, MI

Cooked Millet

3 c. water	½ tsp. salt
1 c. millet	honey (optional)

Bring water to a boil; stir in millet. Boil for 30 minutes. Serve with honey and milk like cornmeal mush.

—Mary E. Beachy, Liberty, KY

Cooked Cereals

Add the following to any hot cereal for variety and a monotony breaker:

1-2 apples, peeled and chopped   a dash of cinnamon
Add apples before cereal and cook until tender.

carob   honey
Mix to a paste and add after cereal.

1 c. raisins
Cook until plump and juicy.

—Mrs. Junior Detweiler, Redding, IA

Cornmeal Mush

3 c. boiling water   **1½ tsp. salt**
1 c. cornmeal   **1 c. cold water or milk**

Mix cornmeal, salt, and 1 c. water. Pour into boiling water, stirring constantly. Cook until thick, then cook over low heat for 10 minutes. Pour into a cake pan and cool. Slice and fry in oil.

—Mrs. Johnny Miller, Loudonville, OH

Wheat Mush

3 c. water   **1¼ c. whole wheat flour**
1 c. cold water   **1 tsp. salt**

Bring 3 c. water to a boil. Combine cold water, whole wheat flour, and salt. Add to boiling water. Stir constantly as mush thickens. A wire whisk works well. Cook 30 minutes, covered, on very low heat or over hot water. Eat hot with milk and honey or pour into loaf pan to cool. Slice, dust with flour, and fry in well greased skillet.

—Cyndi Davis, Flemingsburg, KY

Quick Fried Mush

4 c. cornmeal
2 tsp. salt

¼ c. whole wheat flour
6 c. boiling water

Mix dry ingredients. Add hot water and stir well to mix. Drop by spoonsful in hot greased skillet. Press flat with spatula. If batter gets too thick, add more water. Brown both sides. Serve with liverwurst and ketchup.

—Amelia Troyer, Glenford, OH

Cereal Cake

4 c. oatmeal
2 c. whole wheat flour
1 c. honey
2 tsp. soda

1 tsp. salt
½ c. lard
1 tsp. vanilla or maple flavoring
1¾ c. milk

Bake in a greased cake pan for 30-40 minutes at 350°. Add coconuts, dates, raisins, etc. for a more granola-type cereal. Can be crumbled and toasted same as grapenuts. This is good warm with milk.

—Mrs. Richard Miller, Bremen, IN

Baked Oatmeal

¼ c. butter
2 eggs
½ c. maple syrup
3 c. oatmeal

2 tsp. baking powder
1 tsp. salt
1 c. milk
1 tsp. cinnamon

Mix all together. Put 1 qt. of fruit in glass cake pan and pour batter over fruit. Bake at 350° for 20-30 minutes.

—Mrs. Ervin Bontrager, Hillsboro, WI

Baked Oatmeal

½ tsp. stevia
3 c. oatmeal
2 tsp. baking powder
1 tsp. cinnamon
¼ tsp. nutmeg
¼ tsp. allspice
¼ tsp. cloves

1 tsp. salt
2 eggs
1 tsp. honey
⅓ c. butter
1 c. buttermilk
¾ c. applesauce

Combine dry ingredients thoroughly. Beat eggs and honey until fluffy and add to dry ingredients. Melt butter and add to batter. Last add the buttermilk and applesauce. Mix well and pour into 13" x 9" x 2" or 8" x 12" pan. Bake at 350° for 30 minutes. This has an improved flavor if you mix it the night before and refrigerate it. 45 minutes is needed for baking time then.

—*Mrs. John Houston, Cottage Grove, TN*

Whole Grain Cereal

1 c. rolled oats (not quick)
1 c. bran
½ c. wheat
½ c. barley
½ c. millet
½ c. buckwheat
½ c. rye
1 c. brown rice

½ c. sesame seeds
1 c. almonds
1 c. cashews
1 c. dried prunes
1 c. dried apricots
1 c. raisins
1 c. pumpkin seeds

Cover with water and soak for 12-24 hours. Pureé it or grind it. Slice your favorite fruit on top. No sugar or cream is needed. Store in refrigerator. Will keep indefinitely.

—*Mrs. Dan B. Troyer, Fresno, OH*

High-Fiber Nut Cereal

16 c. oatmeal
4 c. unsweetened coconut
4 c. wheat bran
3 c. honey
2 tsp. salt
2 c. butter

2½ lbs. each of your
choice of: filberts,
almonds, pumpkin seeds,
sesame seeds, or sunflower
seeds (ground fine)

Melt butter and add honey. Add to combined dry ingredients. Mix, spread on cookie sheets, and bake at 250° for 1 hour, stirring every 15 minutes.

—*Mrs. Vernon Hershberger, Loganville, WI*

Healthy Breakfast Cereal

8 c. grapenuts, toasted
6 c. oatmeal
⅓ c. dried apple peelings, crumbled

1 c. raisins
1 c. sunflower seeds

Mix and store in a tight container. This mixture does not need to be toasted.

—*Mrs. Ervin Bontrager, Hillsboro, WI*

And Abraham hastened into the tent unto Sarah and said, Make ready quickly three measures of fine meal, knead it, and make cakes upon the hearth. And Abraham ran unto the herd, and fetched a calf tender and good, and gave it unto a young man; and he hastened to dress it. And he took butter, and milk, and the calf which he had dressed, and set it before them; and he stood by them under the tree, and they did eat.
—*Genesis 18:6-8*

Wheat Germ Crunchies Cereal

2 c. whole wheat flour	3 tsp. baking powder
1 c. wheat germ	2 tsp. cinnamon
1 c. oat bran	3 eggs, beaten
2 c. coconut	1¼ c. butter or olive oil
3 c. oatmeal	1½ tsp. vanilla
1 tsp. salt	1½ tsp. maple flavoring
2 c. honey or sweetener of your choice	

Mix dry ingredients and oil or butter along with eggs and flavorings. Pour onto two cookie sheets and bake at 350° for 20 minutes. After done, crumble and toast the cereal.

—*Mrs. Leroy B. Miller, Middlefield, OH*

Granola

11 qt. oatmeal	1 c. peanut butter
6 c. coconut	1 c. honey or molasses
1 c. sunflower seeds	4½ c. cream or rich milk
raisins or sesame seeds	2 tsp. vanilla
(optional)	1 tsp. soda

In a large bowl, combine oatmeal, coconut, sunflower seeds, and raisins or sesame seeds if desired. In a saucepan, heat and mix peanut butter, honey or molasses, and cream. Add vanilla and soda. Pour onto dry ingredients and mix well. Toast until light brown in a 250° oven, stirring occasionally.

—*Miss Betty Hilty, Oakfield, ME*

People of integrity make an easy target for critics, because they stand upright.

Granola

10 c. rolled oats	1 c. sesame seeds, optional
1½ c. sunflower seeds	1½ c. flaxseed, grind in
1½ c. slivered almonds	blender to a meal
1½ c. wheat germ	⅔ c. honey
1½ c. bran or bran flakes, optional	⅔ c. orange juice
1½ c. unsweetened coconut	2 tsp. vanilla, optional

Mix dry ingredients. In a separate bowl, combine honey, orange juice, and vanilla. Add to dry ingredients. Pour on cookie sheets to dehydrate or bake in 300° oven for 1 hour, stirring occasionally. You may add raisins or other dried fruit if you prefer.

—Sharon Troyer, Millersburg, OH

Granola

4 c. rolled oats	½ c. honey
3 c. quick oats	1 Tbsp. molasses
1 c. freshly ground flour	1 c. applesauce
(rice, wheat, or barley)	¼ c. butter or olive oil
2 c. wheat bran	2 Tbsp. ground flaxseed
1½ c. unsweetened coconut	2 tsp. cinnamon

Mix together dry ingredients. Add oil, honey, molasses, and applesauce and mix well. It should be moist enough that you can make it stick together if you squeeze it in your hand. Bake on cookie sheets or in large roaster at 250°, stirring often, until lightly toasted and dry.

—Irene Mae Yoder, Oakland, MD

Happiness is contagious, spread by a smile.

Grapenuts

7¾ lb. whole wheat flour	3 Tbsp. soda
1½ Tbsp. salt	3 qt. buttermilk
2 c. honey	¾ lb. butter, melted
2 c. maple syrup	

Stir soda into buttermilk, then mix all ingredients except butter. Add that last. Put into 4 greased 9" x 13" pans. Bake at 350° for 1 hour or until well done. The grapenut cakes can either be pushed through a sieve to grate then dried in a 250° oven or they can be cut into strips, dried, and then ground.

—*Mrs. Raymond Fisher, Rebersburg, PA*

Corn Crunch

2 c. buttermilk or sour milk	1 tsp. baking powder
2 c. whole wheat pastry flour	½ tsp. salt
1½ c. cornmeal	¾ c. honey
1 tsp. soda	

Mix all together and bake for 30 minutes in a 375° oven. When cool, crumble and toast like grapenuts.

—*Mrs. Esther Yoder, Hillsboro, WI*

Biscuits and Sausage Gravy

Biscuits:	Gravy:
2 c. whole wheat flour	1 lb. sausage, crumbled
4 tsp. baking powder	4½ c. milk, divided
½ tsp. salt	½ c. whole wheat flour
3 Tbsp. lard	salt and pepper to taste
1¼ c. milk	

Biscuits: Mix flour, baking powder, and salt. Cut in lard. Add milk and stir until thoroughly mixed. Drop by tablespoons on a greased cookie sheet. Bake at 450° for 12 minutes.

Gravy: Brown sausage and add 3½ c. milk. Bring to a boil. Mix 1 c. milk with flour and add to sausage and milk mixture.

—*Mrs. Edward Martin, Alta Vista, IA*

Special Egg Bake

12-16 eggs	bread cubes
¼ c. butter	cheese, bacon, or ham bits

Melt butter in 9" x 13" pan. Arrange bread cubes until bottom is covered. Drop eggs over bread, garnish with fried bacon, ham, or cheese. Add salt and pepper. Bake at 400° for 10 minutes. Reduce heat to 325° and finish to desired doneness. Serve with salsa or hot dog relish.

—*Mrs. Junior Detweiler, Redding, IA*

Breakfast Casserole

1 lb. sausage	1 tsp. salt
6 eggs	1 tsp. dry mustard, optional
2 c. milk	1 c. shredded cheese
6 slices bread, cubed	

Brown and drain sausage. Beat eggs well. Add bread cubes, milk, salt, and mustard. Add sausage and cheese last. Pour into a greased 9" x 9" dish. Bake 45 minutes at 350°. This can be prepared in the evening to be baked the next morning.

—*Thelma Zook, Oakland, MD*

Breakfast Haystack

2 loaves whole wheat bread, cubed and toasted
24 c. potatoes, cooked, peeled, and put through ricer
   when ready to serve

5 doz. eggs, scrambled	5 lbs. ham, cooked and cubed
2 large onions, minced	8 qt. cheese sauce

Each person builds their own haystack, (stacking one item on top of the other) on their plate in order given and top with cheese sauce.

—*Mrs. Vernon Hershberger, Loganville, WI*

Potato-Cheese Omelet

3 Tbsp. butter
¼ c. chopped onion
1 c. sliced cooked potatoes
6 eggs
¼ c. milk

⅓ c. diced green peppers
½ c. shredded Cheddar cheese
¼ c. dried thyme
dash paprika
fresh parsley

Heat butter in cast-iron skillet. Add onions and potatoes. Cook and stir until potatoes are golden. Beat eggs and add milk. Stir in peppers, cheese, and thyme. Pour over potatoes. Cook over low heat till set. Fold omelet and put on plate. Top with paprika and parsley.

—*Mrs. Leroy Auker, Elk Horn, KY*

Breakfast Skillet

2-3 Tbsp. butter
2 c. potatoes, shredded
salt and pepper
crumbled bacon, sausage, or diced ham

5 eggs, beaten
¼ c. milk
grated cheese

Melt butter in a large preheated stainless steel skillet. Add potatoes, stir to coat, and sprinkle with salt and pepper to taste. Fry for 5 minutes over medium heat; turn potatoes and pour eggs and milk over them. Sprinkle on grated cheese as desired and crumbled bacon, sausage, or diced ham. Keep over low-medium heat until eggs are set. Serve immediately.

—*Amanda Bricker, Cass City, MI*

A song a day keeps the blues away. It's pretty hard to be downhearted when one is singing a cheery tune.

Breads, Rolls, Muffins, & Biscuits

Wholesome Grains

Most people interested in healthy eating know that whole grains are much more nutritious than refined grains such as bleached flours and white rice. It is very important, however, for these whole grains to be properly prepared for your body to get the maximum benefits possible.

Most grains, nuts, and seeds contain enzyme inhibitors and phytic acid that block absorption of minerals such as calcium and magnesium. This problem can be easily corrected by using various soaking methods such as using sourdough in baking and partially germinating seeds before grinding.

Eating germinated grains not only strengthens your natural digestive tract enzymes, but also boosts the vitamin content. Partially germinated seeds contain considerably more vitamins B and C and dramatically increase carotene levels (commonly known as vitamin A). Many people who are allergic to refined wheat products have been helped by eating germinated grains. Use of a different grain, such as spelt or rye, may also be helpful.

Our method of germinating wheat berries and preparing for grinding (also known as bulgur wheat):
Fill wide-mouth quart jars ⅓ full of hard winter wheat berries. Fill completely with water and let set at room temperature for 8-12 hours or until at least half of the berries are just barely sprouted; drain, rinse with fresh water, and drain completely. Place a thin layer on cookie sheets or screens. Put in oven on low heat overnight or until completely dry. Grind into flour. (Berries that haven't been totally dried will clog your grinder.) This will make a most nutritious flour that you can feel good about feeding your family.

Flour should be ground fresh and kept in a cool place. The wheat germ oil in whole wheat flour spoils rather quickly after grinding.

Homemade Bread

Mix together:	In another bowl mix:
5½ c. warm water	1 c. warm water
2 Tbsp. salt	1 tsp. honey
½ c. oil	¼ c. yeast
½ c. honey	Let rise until bubbly then
4 eggs	add to other mixture.

Add 8 c. whole wheat flour; stir well. Add 6-7 c. more flour. Knead for 10 minutes or until dough comes off knuckles. Let rise for 2 hours. Punch down, divide into 6 parts, shape into loaves, and let rise until nearly double in size. Bake at 350° for 45 minutes.

—*Loveda Bear, Patriot, OH*

Whole Wheat Bread

1½ c. warm water	¾ c. soft lard
1½ Tbsp. sorghum	1½ Tbsp. salt
3 Tbsp. yeast	4 eggs, beaten
3 c. warm water	14 c. wheat flour
¾ c. honey or sorghum	

Combine and dissolve first 3 ingredients. Let rise. Combine rest of ingredients except flour. Add yeast mixture. Stir. Add flour. Knead 10 minutes after last flour is added. Cover and let rise in a warm place for one hour. Punch down and let rise another hour. Punch down again and let rise 1½-2 hours. Work out into 1¼-lb. loaves. Let rise in a warm place, covered, until 2½"-3" above pan. If dough is a bit too sticky, don't allow to rise as long, as it tends to flatten when too sticky. Bake for 25-30 minutes at 370°.

—*Alma Rhodes, Scottsville, KY*

Delicious Whole Wheat Bread

3 Tbsp. yeast	¼ c. olive oil or coconut oil
⅓ c. maple syrup or honey	8 c. (heaping) whole
4 c. warm water	wheat flour
⅓ c. vinegar	1 tsp. salt

Mix water, maple syrup or honey, vinegar, and yeast in a bowl. Let set for 15 minutes or until yeast has worked (becomes spongy or bubbly). Then add salt and oil. Add flour, 3-4 c., and mix well; then add 1 c. at a time until rest of flour is stirred in and it's a spongy soft dough. If it's not spongy, the bread won't be nice and soft. Set dough in a warm place (not hot) till ready to work out. Let rise; punch down every 10 minutes or so. Punch down 3 times. Do not let rise longer than 1 hour before putting in pans or it won't rise well in pans. Divide into 4 pans and prick with fork. Set in a warm place and let rise till edges of loaf reaches top of pans. Bake for 30 minutes, starting at 350° for a little bit then close to 400° until it's done.

—*Mrs. Abie J. Troyer, Ashland, OH*

Sourdough Starter

2 c. flour	1 c. cooled potato water
2 c. water	1 Tbsp. yeast

Mix well and let set in a warm area until it is done fermenting. (It will separate and no more bubles are present.) Stir well, remove 1 c. of the contents and stir in another cup of flour and 1 c. water. The new starter is ready to use after 3-4 days. The sourdough flavor will improve as your starter ages. Feed your starter several times a week. Always remove 1 c. starter then add 1 c. flour and 1 c. water or enough to make it soupy. Do not refrigerate. Leave it on the counter. Potato water is the water you boil potatoes in.

—*Mrs. Ellen Murphy, Pearisburg, VA*

Sourdough Bread

2 c. starter
1 c. milk
¼ c. butter
¼ c. honey

2 tsp. salt
2 tsp. soda
5-7 c. flour

Scald milk; stir butter, honey, and salt into milk and cool to lukewarm. Add sourdough starter. Dissolve soda in 1 Tbsp. warm water and stir in. Add flour until dough is kneadable. Knead well. Let rise approximately 3 hours. When doubled, punch down and shape into 2 loaves. Place in greased loaf pans and let rise until the hump is above edges of pans. Bake at 400° for 25-30 minutes. Rising times will vary with temperature and strength of starter.

—*Mrs. Ellen Murphy, Pearisburg, VA*

Tomato Bread

1 c. tomato juice
¼ c. butter
1 c. water
2 tsp. salt
1 Tbsp. honey
Cook together and cool
to lukewarm.

Add:
1 Tbsp. yeast, dissolved in
½ c. warm water
2 eggs, beaten
1½ c. oat flour or whole
wheat flour

Mix well and add approximately 5 c. whole wheat flour to make a soft dough. Let rise until double, punch down, and work out into buns or loaves. Let rise until double in size. Bake at 350° for 30 minutes.

—*Thelma Zook, Oakland, MD*

*When converting a recipe use ¾ c. whole
grain flour for 1 c. white flour.*

Frieden Herb Bread

2 pkg. yeast	1 c. milk
¼ c. warm water	½ c. honey
2 tsp. salt	5 c. whole wheat flour
¼ c. butter or lard	2 eggs
½ tsp. dried basil	½ tsp. dried thyme
½ tsp. dried oregano	1 tsp. nutmeg

Soften yeast in warm water. Scald milk; measure honey, salt, and butter into bowl; add milk. Cool. Add 2 c. flour. Beat and add yeast and eggs, slightly beaten. Add herbs and flour to make soft dough. If using ground herbs, use less than if herbs are leaves. Knead and let rise like other bread. Bake at 350° for 30 minutes.

—*Thelma Zook, Oakland, MD*

Wholesome Harvest Bread

½ c. yellow cornmeal	½ c. warm water
½ c. honey	1 c. rye flour
¼ c. oil	1 c. whole wheat flour
1 Tbsp. salt	1 c. toasted sunflower seeds
2 c. boiling water	¼ c. poppy seeds
2 Tbsp. yeast	3 c. whole wheat flour

Mix together cornmeal, honey, oil, and salt. Pour water over this mixture; let set to cool. Dissolve yeast in ½ c. water and add to cooled mixture. Add rye and 1 c. wheat flour and beat well. Add the seeds. Mix well, then finish with whole wheat flour. Let rise, punch down, and divide into 2 loaves. Let rise until almost double. Bake at 350° for 45 minutes.

—*Mary E. Showalter, Mt. Solon, VA*

Oatmeal Molasses Bread

1½ c. boiling water	2 Tbsp. active dry yeast
1 c. rolled oats	½ c. warm water
⅓ c. butter or olive oil	2 eggs, beaten
½ c. sorghum	5-6 c. whole wheat flour
1 Tbsp. salt	

Mix the first five ingredients together. Cool to lukewarm. Combine dry yeast and ½ c. warm water. Stir into lukewarm oatmeal mixture. Mix well. Add eggs and flour. Mix thoroughly. Cover; let stand for 15 minutes. Turn onto well floured board; shape into 2 loaves. Let rise in a warm place in bread pans until double (about 1½ hour). Bake at 350° for 1 hour or until brown.

—*Mary Showalter, Mt. Solon, VA*

Mini Garlic Breads

6 Tbsp. soft butter	½ tsp. Italian seasoning
⅔ tsp. dill weed	½ tsp. onion powder
½ tsp. garlic powder	Italian bread

Combine first five ingredients, stirring well. Spread on bread slices. Place on baking sheet. Broil until golden.

—*Mary Detweiler, West Farmington, OH*

Garlic Bread

1 loaf bread	1 tsp. parsley flakes
1 stick butter	Parmesan cheese
½ tsp. oregano	garlic salt

Mix butter, oregano, and parsley flakes. Slice bread in 1" slices. Spread with butter mixture and sprinkle with Parmesan cheese and garlic salt. Put loaf together, wrap in foil, and heat. Use garlic salt a little sparingly as it gets too salty.

—*Mrs. Edward Martin, Alta Vista, IA*

Spoon Bread

1 pt. sweet milk
6 Tbsp. butter
1 c. cornmeal

1 tsp. salt
3 eggs, separated and at
    room temperature

Scald milk (do not boil). Stir in butter, cornmeal, and salt. Cook, stirring constantly, until cornmeal comes away from the sides of the pan and thickens. Set aside to cool to lukewarm. Add beaten egg yolks; mix thoroughly. Fold in stiffly beaten egg whites; mix gently but thoroughly. Pour into greased and floured 2-qt. baking dish. Bake at 375° for 1 hour or until top is golden brown. Serve immediately. Yield: 6 servings.

—Jolene Bontrager, Hillsboro, WI

Maple Syrup Corn Bread

1⅓ c. whole wheat pastry flour
⅔ c. cornmeal (or corn flour)
3 tsp. baking powder
½ tsp. sea salt (optional)

2 eggs, beaten
⅔ c. milk
⅓ c. maple syrup
½ c. oil

Mix dry ingredients. Add eggs, milk, syrup, and oil. Mix and pour into an 8" or 9" round pan. Bake at 375° for 25-30 minutes or until a toothpick inserted into the center comes out clean.

—Mrs. DaWayne Hochstetler, Nappanee, IN

> *Therefore the Lord himself shall give you a sign; behold, a virgin shall conceive, and bear a son, and shall call his name Immanuel. Butter and honey shall he eat, that he may know to refuse the evil, and choose the good.*
>
> *—Isaiah 7:14-15*

Quin's Favorite Corn Bread

2 c. whole wheat flour
2 c. yellow cornmeal
½ c. honey
6 tsp. baking powder
2 tsp. salt

2 c. applesauce or pureed
   pumpkin
2 c. milk
2 eggs, beaten

Mix dry ingredients. Add liquids and mix well. Pour into a greased 11" x 13" pan. Bake 20 minutes at 450°.

Variation: Use 5 tsp. baking powder and 1 tsp. soda with buttermilk (instead of milk). Pour into 2 greased cast-iron skillets. Bake in oven or cover with foil and cook over low temperature (set stove top on medium-low) until firm or about 20-25 minutes. Watch carefully. Can also be baked on top of a woodstove over a warm, not hot, area of stove to prevent burning. Yield: 16 servings.

—*Cyndi Davis, Flemingsburg, KY*

Oatmeal Pone

2 c. rolled oats
1 c. whole wheat flour
1 tsp. baking soda
1 tsp. salt

¼ c. or less natural sweetener

1 egg
1¼ c. milk, cream, or sour
   milk

Blend dry ingredients. Add sweetener, egg, and milk. Bake in an 8" square pan at 350° for 30 minutes or until done.

Variation: Add approximately ¾ c. chopped apples to the batter.

—*Mrs. Urie R. Miller, Shipshewana, IN*

Those who say "work well done never needs redoing" never weeded a garden.

Oatmeal Shortbread

3½ c. oatmeal	⅓ c. olive oil
¼ c. whole wheat flour	½ tsp. salt
⅓ c. honey	1 tsp. cinnamon

Mix all ingredients together to make a stiff dough. Oil and flour a 9" x 13" pan. Press dough firmly into pan. Bake at 325° until light brown or about 30 minutes. Cool for 10 minutes, then cut into squares.

—Laura Royer, Camden, IN

Banana Bread

8 c. whole grain flour	1½ c. nuts
2½ tsp. stevia	8 eggs
6 tsp. soda	6 c. bananas
3 tsp. salt	1½ c. butter
2 tsp. cinnamon	2 Tbsp. honey
1 tsp. nutmeg	2 tsp. vanilla

Combine dry ingredients thoroughly. Cream rest of ingredients, mix together well, and pour into 6 bread pans. Bake at 275° for 1 hour.

—Mrs. John Houston, Cottage Grove, TN

Banana Bread

2 c. whole wheat flour	2 eggs
1 tsp. baking soda	½ c. honey
½ tsp. salt	¼ c. oil
1 tsp. cinnamon	½ tsp. vanilla
2 c. ripe bananas, mashed	½ c. nuts, chopped

Mix wet ingredients together, then add dry ingredients. Mix well. Pour into greased large bread pan. Bake at 275° for 1 hour.

—Mrs. Raymond Yutzy, Howe, IN

Zucchini Bread

3 tsp. cinnamon	3 tsp. vanilla
3 eggs	2 c. grated zucchini
1 c. olive oil	⅔ c. chopped nuts
¼ tsp. baking powder	3 c. whole wheat flour
1 c. honey	1 tsp. soda

Mix oil, honey, vanilla, eggs, and grated zucchini. Mix lightly but well. Add flour, soda, cinnamon, and baking powder. Mix until blended; add nuts. Pour into 2 greased bread pans. Bake at 325° for 1 hour. Remove and cool on rack.

—*Jolene Bontrager, Hillsboro, WI*

Multi-Grain Date Loaf

1 c. boiling water	1 c. whole wheat flour
1 c. dates, chopped	1 tsp. baking powder
1 tsp. baking soda	¼ tsp. salt
1 c. oatmeal	½ c. maple syrup
1 c. bran	½ c. milk

Pour the boiling water over the dates and baking soda. Let stand. Mix oatmeal, bran, whole wheat flour, baking powder, and salt together. Add maple syrup, milk, and date mixture. Pour into a loaf pan that has been lined with waxed paper. Bake at 325° or less for 35 minutes, turning every 10 minutes so it does not burn.

—*Elizabeth Drudge, Wroxeter, Ontario*

A smile is the prettiest thing you'll ever wear.

Apple Gingerbread

1 Tbsp. butter
5 apples, sliced
½ c. maple syrup
3 Tbsp. butter
½ c. sorghum
1½ c. whole wheat flour

¾ tsp. cinnamon
¾ tsp. ginger
¼ tsp. allspice
1 tsp. soda
½ c. sour milk or buttermilk

Brown 1 Tbsp. butter in an iron skillet, add sliced apples and maple syrup. Simmer a few minutes. Mix the rest of the ingredients and pour on top of the apples. Cover and bake on top of the stove over low heat. Eat warm with milk.

—*Malinda Yoder, Marion, KY*

Gingerbread

½ c. molasses
1 tsp. soda
½ c. butter
3 eggs
3 c. whole grain flour
1½ tsp. cinnamon

1 tsp. stevia
½ tsp. ginger
½ tsp. nutmeg
1 tsp. soda
1 c. buttermilk
1 tsp. vanilla

Beat molasses and soda until foamy. Add butter and eggs and beat well. In a separate bowl, combine dry ingredients except soda thoroughly. Add to beaten mixture. Dissolve soda in buttermilk and add to rest of batter. Add vanilla and mix until smooth. Pour into an 8" x 12" pan and bake at 350° for 45 minutes. Top warm gingerbread with whipped cream and enjoy!

—*Mrs. John Houston, Cottage Grove, TN*

Gingerbread

1 c. maple syrup
2 c. Prairie Gold® flour
½ tsp. salt
1 tsp. soda

1 c. sour milk
1 egg
1 tsp. ginger or cinnamon

Mix together dry ingredients. Beat egg, then add syrup and sour milk. Stir in dry ingredients. Bake at 350° for 50 minutes or until done.

—*Mrs. Neil Byler, Bellville, OH*

Applesauce Bread

½ c. soft butter
2 eggs
1 tsp. vanilla
2 c. whole wheat flour
1 tsp. baking powder
1 tsp. soda
¾ tsp. salt

2 tsp. cinnamon
½ tsp. nutmeg
½ tsp. stevia
1 c. applesauce
1 c. raisins
½ c. water

Cream butter, eggs, and vanilla together until fluffy. In a separate bowl, combine dry ingredients thoroughly. Mix with butter-egg mixture. Cook raisins in water for 5 minutes. Add this and applesauce to other ingredients and beat well. Pour into greased loaf pan and let set 20 minutes (to enhance flavor). Bake at 350° for 1 hour or till done. Cool, wrap, and store in fridge.

—*Mrs. John Houston, Cottage Grove, TN*

Commit thy works unto the Lord, and thy thoughts shall be established.
—*Proverbs 16:3*

Very Best Buns

2 Tbsp. yeast
2 c. water
¼ c. soft butter
⅓ c. honey

2 eggs, beaten
6 c. flour
2 tsp. salt

Dissolve yeast in water. Add butter, honey, and eggs. Blend in flour and salt. Let rise as for bread. Roll out ¾" thick. Cut with wide-mouth jar or pineapple can. Bake at 325° for 25 minutes or until lightly browned on the bottom. Slice them in half like hamburger buns. Can also use as bread.

Note: These don't keep as long as bread. Freeze if you don't use them soon.

—*Linda Yoder, Pleasant Hill, IL*

Jiffy Hamburger Buns

4-4½ c. whole wheat flour
2 Tbsp. yeast
1 c. milk
¾ c. water

½ c. oil
3 Tbsp. honey
1 tsp. salt

Stir together 2 c. flour and yeast. Heat milk, water, oil, honey, and salt until very warm (120°-130°). Pour into yeast and flour mixture. Beat 300 strokes by hand. Add remaining flour to make a soft dough. Beat well or knead briefly. Let rise 10 minutes. Roll out ½" thick on floured surface. Cut into 3" or 4" rounds with jar ring or tuna can. Let rise on greased baking sheets for ½ hour. Bake at 400° until lightly browned or for 12-15 minutes. Yield: 12-15.

—*Eva Troyer, Scottsville, KY*

Cinnamon Buns

Make your favorite whole wheat bread dough. Let rise once, then shape into balls the size of a walnut. Roll in melted butter then honey and cinnamon. Place on a 13" x 9" cake pan and let rise until almost double. Bake at 350° for 35 minutes or until done. Use only the desired amount of dough and make the rest into loaves of bread.

—*Mrs. Vernon Hershberger, Loganville, WI*

Pecan Rolls

½ c. maple syrup
½ c. water

2 Tbsp. butter
1 c. chopped pecans

In a saucepan, heat maple syrup, water, and butter. Pour into a 9" x 13" cake pan. Sprinkle pecans into syrup. Using your favorite bread dough, roll out dough ½" thick on a greased surface. Spread rolled out dough with butter, sprinkle sucanat to coat evenly, then sprinkle generously with cinnamon. Roll dough together and cut. Place in pan on top of nuts and syrup. Let rise until almost double. Bake at 350° for 20 minutes. Invert on a large plate to cool.

—*Mrs. Raymond Yutzy, Howe, IN*

Love not the world, neither the things that are in the world. If any man love the world, the love of the Father is not in him.
—I John 2:15

100% Whole Wheat Sticky Buns

3 c. warm water
1¾ Tbsp. yeast
1 Tbsp. salt

½ c. honey
2 eggs, beaten
8-9 c. whole wheat flour

Mix water, yeast, salt, and honey and let set until yeast is dissolved. Add eggs. Add 4 c. flour, beat well, and add 4 more. Add more flour as needed. Let rise 30 minutes. Work down. Repeat every 30 minutes 4 times. Roll out and spread with butter. Sprinkle with cinnamon and nuts as desired. Roll up and cut 1" slices and put in pans with maple syrup in the bottom. Bake at 275° for 45 minutes or until done.

Variation: Raisins may be added if desired.

—*Mary Nolt, Withee, WI*

Jelly Roll

5 eggs, separated
5 Tbsp. water
½ c. honey (slightly warmed)
1 tsp. flavoring

1 c. spelt flour
1 tsp. baking powder
½ tsp. salt

Separate the eggs. Beat the whites. In another bowl beat the yolks, water, honey, and flavoring until fluffy. Add flour, baking powder, and salt. Last add the beaten egg whites. Mix gently. Bake in a jelly roll pan lined with waxed paper. Bake at 400° for 10-12 minutes.

—*Mrs. Reuben Miller, Millersburg, OH*

A day without bread is a long one indeed.

Banana Muffins

1 c. whole wheat flour
½ c. oatmeal
1 egg, beaten
¼ c. oil
½ tsp. cinnamon
¾ c. raisins

1 tsp. baking powder
1 tsp. soda
½ tsp. salt
1½ c. ripe bananas or
    crushed pineapple

Mix all dry ingredients together. In a separate bowl, mix wet ingredients well. Mix both mixtures together. Put in greased muffin tins. Bake at 400° for 20-25 minutes. Yield: 1 dozen.

—*Mrs. Ivan Yoder, Ashland, OH*

Oatmeal Raisin Muffins

1 c. whole wheat flour
1 c. old-fashioned rolled oats
1 tsp. baking soda
¼ c. honey
1 tsp. cinnamon
⅛ tsp. cloves

½ tsp. salt
½ c. raisins
1 egg, beaten
1 c. buttermilk or yogurt
3 Tbsp. olive oil
¼ c. water

Mix all dry ingredients thoroughly, including raisins. Make a well in the center and add honey, egg, milk, oil, and water. Mix only till dry ingredients are moist. Fill greased muffin pans half full and bake at 375° for 15 minutes. Good hot or cold and freezes well. Yield: 12-16 muffins.

Variations: Substitute 1 c. blueberries or chopped fruit for raisins.

—*Cyndi Davis, Flemingsburg, KY*

When looking for faults use a mirror, not a telescope.

Buttermilk Oatmeal Muffins

1 c. rolled oats	1 c. whole wheat flour
1 c. buttermilk	½ tsp. salt
1 egg	1 tsp. soda
¼ c. warm honey	⅓ c. olive oil

Soak oats in buttermilk at least 30 minutes. Beat egg into oat mixture. Add honey and mix well. Stir flour, salt, and soda together. Stir into first mixture. Then add oil and mix only until ingredients are mixed. Bake in buttered muffin pan for 15-20 minutes at 425°. Yield: 1 dozen.

—*Jolene Bontrager, Hillsboro, WI*

Cinnamuffins

¼ c. oil	1½ tsp. baking powder
½ c. dark molasses	¾ tsp. cinnamon
1 c. applesauce	½ tsp. salt
1½ c. flour	½ c. raisins
½ tsp. soda	

Preheat oven to 375°. Line muffin tins with paper cups. Mix oil, molasses, and applesauce. Sift together flour, soda, baking powder, cinnamon, and salt. Stir together wet and dry ingredients; add raisins. Drop into muffin cups and bake for 18-20 minutes. Yield: 12 small muffins or 8-10 large muffins.

—*Laura Yoder, Free Union, VA*

I believe a higher power (God) programmed our food to naturally give us good health and we have lost sight of His handiwork.
—*Allan Nation*

Cinnamon-Topped Oatmeal Muffins

1 c. whole wheat flour	1 egg
¼ tsp. stevia	4 Tbsp. butter
1 Tbsp. baking powder	1 tsp. honey
½ tsp. salt	1 c. milk or buttermilk
1 c. oats	1 tsp. vanilla
½ c. raisins	

Combine dry ingredients and raisins thoroughly. Whip the egg. Beat butter and honey till fluffy. Add milk and vanilla to butter mixture. Add dry ingredients. Add the egg last and mix well. Sprinkle with crumbs. Bake for 15 minutes in preheated 400° oven. Yield: 1 dozen.

Crumbs:

2 Tbsp. date sugar or 1 tsp. honey	
2 Tbsp. flour	½ tsp. baking powder
⅓ c. oats	4 Tbsp. butter, melted
1 tsp. cinnamon	

Combine dry ingredients and combine wet ingredients, then mix all together.

—Mrs. John Houston, Cottage Grove, TN

A scoutmaster told his cub scouts to remember "that in the woods we are the guests of the animals and trees and plants." I like that!

A refined person is very careful of the house and furniture where he is being entertained. He handles objects with even more care than if they were his own. Likewise, as guests of God, we are courtesy-bound to conserve the resources of God's good earth, its forests, its soil, its oil, its water power, that we may leave to our posterity a land richer than we found. We...sometimes act as if our country's wealth was inexhaustible and also wholly our own. Not so!... "The earth is the Lord's and the fullness thereof." Let us not forget that basic truth.

Molasses Muffins

2 c. whole wheat flour	¼ c. oil
2 tsp. baking powder	½ c. molasses
1 egg	½ c. raisins
½ c. milk	

Preheat oven to 400°. Butter a 12-cup muffin tin. In a medium bowl combine flour and baking powder. In a small bowl, mix egg, milk, oil, molasses, and raisins. Blend. Add to dry ingredients and mix till moist. Fill muffin cups two-thirds full. Bake for 15-20 minutes. Yield: 1 dozen.

—*Mrs. Leroy Auker, Elk Horn, KY*

Gingerbread Muffins

2 c. whole wheat pastry flour	⅓ c. sorghum
1 tsp. baking powder	⅔ c. honey
1 tsp. soda	⅓ c. olive oil
1 Tbsp. ginger	1 egg
1½ tsp. cinnamon	1 c. water
½ tsp. cloves	¾ c. quick oats

Combine all dry ingredients except oats and separately combine liquid ingredients. Stir wet mixture into dry mixture, mixing very little, then mix in oats. Stir briefly; do not beat. Spoon batter into paper-lined or greased muffin cups. Bake in a preheated 350° oven for 15 minutes or until done. Yield: 16 muffins.

—*Laura Royer, Camden, IN*

In the choice between changing one's mind and proving there's no need to do so, most people get busy on the proof.
—*John Kenneth Galbraith*

Boston Blueberry Muffins

1 tsp. honey
½ c. butter
2 eggs
2 c. whole grain flour
2 tsp. baking powder
½ tsp. salt

½ tsp. stevia
¾ tsp. cinnamon
1 tsp. vanilla
5 Tbsp. applesauce
2½ c. blueberries

Cream butter and honey until fluffy. Whip eggs in separate bowl. Combine dry ingredients thoroughly and add to butter mixture. Add vanilla and applesauce, then the eggs. Fold blueberries in last. Sprinkle with streusel topping. Pour into greased muffin tins and bake at 350° for 12-18 minutes.

Streusel Topping:
¼ c. date sugar
⅓ c. whole grain flour
1 tsp. cinnamon

¼ c. butter, melted
½ c. oatmeal

Combine dry ingredients. Cut in melted butter until crumbly. Variation: 1 Tbsp. honey may be substituted for the date sugar.

—*Mrs. John Houston, Cottage Grove, TN*

Cornmeal Biscuits

1 c. cornmeal
1 c. whole wheat flour
1 Tbsp. baking powder
½ tsp. salt

3 Tbsp. butter or oil
1 egg
¾ c. milk

Mix together cornmeal, flour, baking powder, and salt. Cut in butter. Add egg and milk. Drop on stew and bake 15-20 minutes at 375°, covered or uncovered.

—*Mrs. Esther Yoder, Hillsboro, WI*

Biscuits (for top of stew)

1 c. cornmeal
2 c. whole wheat flour
½ c. butter
2 eggs

1 c. milk
1 tsp. salt
4 tsp. baking powder

Using a fork, mix cornmeal, flour, and butter until crumbly and well mixed. Add the rest of ingredients and stir together only until everything is mixed. Have 2-3 qt. of boiling soup or stew ready in a roaster. Stew should have plenty of liquid. Drop biscuits by teaspoonful on stew and return to baking oven. Bake at 375° until browned.

—*Jolene Bontrager, Hillsboro, WI*

Sour Cream Biscuits

2 c. whole wheat flour
1 tsp. soda
1 tsp. sea salt

¼ c. wheat germ
1½ c. sour cream

Sift flour, soda, and salt together. Add wheat germ; fold in sour cream. Knead lightly on floured bread board. Roll ½" thick and cut with biscuit cutter. Place biscuits in a greased pan. Bake in preheated 475° oven for 12-15 minutes.

—*Mary S. Yoder, Wooster, OH*

I will praise thee; for I am fearfully and wonderfully made: marvelous are thy works; and that my soul knoweth right well.
—*Psalm 139:14*

Melt-in-your-Mouth Biscuits

1 egg
⅔ c. milk
2 Tbsp. sweetener
2 c. whole wheat flour

1 Tbsp. baking powder
1 tsp. salt
½ c. butter or homemade lard

Mix all ingredients together lightly. Drop by tablespoons and bake at 375°-400° until crunchy brown or for 10-15 minutes. Serve with sugar-free apple butter or tomato gravy and homemade sausage.

Variation: You can substitute cornmeal or quick oats for part of the flour.

—Mrs. Junior Detweiler, Redding, IA

Whole Wheat Buttermilk Biscuits

2 c. whole wheat flour
1 tsp. soda
½ tsp. salt

⅓ c. butter or lard
1 c. buttermilk

Use finely ground flour and stir it well to lighten it. Mix flour, soda, and salt. Cut in butter or lard. Add buttermilk. Mix thoroughly, but do not overmix. Pat into ¾" thickness on floured board or cookie sheet. Cut biscuits and if desired dip in melted butter. Bake at 425° for 15 20 minutes. To save time, biscuits may be dropped.

—Mrs. J. T., Hestand, KY

> *Do we want tolerance or do we want truth?*
> *—Seen on a church sign*

Whole Wheat Bread Hints:

• Do not add too much flour when kneading the dough. Use just enough to keep from sticking. Whole wheat dough will be somewhat sticky – dough should be bouncy but soft. Too much flour makes it tough and hard and the resulting bread will be dry and crumbly.

• Do not let bread dough rise more than double at any point. That would cause the texture to be more full of holes and more coarse and crumbly.

• Right after forming, prick loaves with a fork to keep air bubbles from forming.

• Whole wheat bread spoils quickly. To freshen a loaf going stale, wrap in tinfoil or a dampened paper bag and place in a warm oven until heated through. Remove from wrapping and cover with a cloth to cool. Replace in plastic bag.

• The quality of your bread will depend a lot on the quality of the flour you use.

Know ye not that ye are the temple of the Lord, and that the Spirit dwelleth in you? If any man defile the temple of God, him shall God destroy; for the temple of God is holy, which temple ye are.
—I Corinthians 3:16-17

Shakes, Smoothies, & Beverages

Soy

Have we all heard that soy is so good for us? Have we heard that soybeans are full of vitamins and proteins? Are we thinking that the more soy products we eat and drink, the better off we are? Much research has been done, and this research is showing facts that are very disturbing.

Soybeans have plant compounds that act like estrogen, a female hormone. Women use soy products to help problems caused by hormonal imbalances. So think about what soy products do to people in all other stages of life who do *not* need the estrogen hormone. Babies, little boys and girls, young women, and all men will also certainly be affected by any soy products they take.

Phytoestrogens, found in soy, cause adult levels of hormones in small children. This can cause an imbalance in many of their organs and glands such as the pituitary, thyroid, adrenal glands, and others.

Soy is highly allergenic (which means it can cause allergies). It is an ingredient found in hundreds of prepared foods, drinks, baby formulas, and even vitamins and health care products. Sometimes soy will not even be mentioned in a certain product's ingredients. It will just be labeled as natural flavorings or ingredients.

Soy products are probably the most overrated so-called health product on the market today, but these products have been causing epidemic levels of thyroid problems and hormone imbalances. The traditional soy products that Asian societies consume have usually gone through a long slow fermentation. These are used in small amounts as a condiment.

MSG

MSG is a neurotoxic substance that may cause nervous system reactions ranging from headaches to permanent brain damage. MSG is found in over 90% of our processed foods. Hydrolyzed protein, malt flavorings, and natural flavorings often contain MSG.

Fruity Breakfast Drink

4 c. orange juice
2 frozen bananas, quartered
1 c. unsweetened frozen
  strawberries
1 c. unsweetened frozen
  raspberries
2 tsp. honey

Combine all ingredients in a blender or Salsa Master until smooth. Yield: 7 c.

—Mrs. Naomi Ruth Bontrager, Mio, MI

Strawberry Shake

8 oz. strawberries
2 c. milk
1 tsp. vanilla
½ tsp. stevia
1 whole banana, frozen

Put in blender in order given. Blend on high. Add milk for desired thickness.

Variations: Add any fruit of your choice. Peaches – add ⅛ tsp. nutmeg. Blueberries – add ½ tsp. lemon juice. Raspberries – go well with bananas. Peanut butter – ¼ c. natural peanut butter and 2 bananas frozen whole.

—Mrs. John Houston, Cottage Grove, TN

Strawberry Breakfast

1 c. fresh or fozen strawberries
½ c. milk
¼ c. plain yogurt
2 Tbsp. lemon juice
2 Tbsp. honey
1 c. ice cubes

Whirl in blender. Add ice cubes 1 at a time and blend thoroughly.

—Iva Kauffman, Monroe, WI

Blueberry Smoothie

1 c. blueberries
2 peaches

1 frozen banana
1 c. orange or apple juice

Whirl all ingredients in blender until smooth.

—*Erma Hoover, Penn Yan, NY*

Pineapple Cranberry Shake

1 c. pineapple
1 banana
1 c. cranberry juice

½ c. yogurt
¼ c. honey
2 c. ice

Put all ingredients in blender except ice. Add ice slowly, blending thoroughly.

—*Iva Kauffman, Monroe, WI*

Best-Ever Shake

2 bananas
½ c. freshly grated coconut
dash cinnamon
½ c. cantaloupe

1 c. unsweetened applesauce
sprigs of mint
1 papaya
1 c. plain or vanilla yogurt

Pour all ingredients into a blender and blend until smooth.

—*Mrs. Leroy B. Miller, Middlefield, OH*

A simple way to get bananas ready for recipes using frozen bananas – peel, drop into a freezer bag, and freeze.

Two-Fruit Frosty

1½ c. fresh or frozen blueberries ¼-⅓ c. honey
   or huckleberres   ½ tsp. ground cinnamon
1 c. frozen unsweetened sliced ½ tsp. ground nutmeg
   peaches, thawed   cinnamon sticks, optional
1 c. milk or 1 c. (8 oz.) vanilla yogurt

Combine buleberries or huckleberries, peaches, and milk in a blender, cover, and process on high. Add milk or yogurt, honey, cinnamon, and nutmeg; blend well. Pour into glasses. Garnish with cinnamon sticks if desired. Serve immediately. Yield: 4 (1 c.) servings.

—*Mrs. Leroy B. Miller, Middlefield, OH*

Carob Shake

3 Tbsp. carob powder   1 c. cold milk
¼ c. honey   ½ tsp. vanilla
2 bananas   ¼ tsp. cinnamon

Whirl in blender until thoroughly blended.

—*Iva Kauffman, Monroe, WI*

Banana Slush

6 oz. frozen orange juice   1 can crushed pineapple
2 c. water   8 sliced or mashed bananas

Freeze.

—*Mrs. Mervin H. Yoder, Pleasant Hill, IL*

Mint Tea

10 c. water
½ tsp. stevia

1 Tbsp. dried and minced
spearmint leaves

Process in an electric coffeemaker. Add stevia to hot tea, then pour over ice and add water to make one gallon.

—*Mrs. John Houston, Cottage Grove, TN*

Almond Milk

Soak almonds in water to cover overnight. Blend on high for a couple minutes and put through sieve.

—*Mrs. David Weaver, Millersburg, OH*

Hot Ginger Tea

1 Tbsp. finely grated ginger   2 c. boiling water
honey, agave nectar, stevia extract powder or liquid to taste

Place ginger in a tea infuser in a small nonmetallic teapot. Add the water and steep, covered, for 15 minutes. Remove the tea infuser and serve with one of the sweeteners listed above.

—*Mrs. Leroy B. Miller, Middlefield, OH*

Sleepy Tea

1½ c. orange segments
2 Tbsp. frozen orange juice
    concentrate
pinch of ground cloves
1 Tbsp. fresh lemon juice

2 tsp. honey
2 pinches ground cinnamon
2 c. strong brewed
    chamomile tea made
    into cubes and crushed

Blend all together.

—*Mrs. Leroy B. Miller, Middlefield, OH*

Gardener's Lemonade

⅓ c. sweetener   1 Tbsp. fresh lemon balm
3 c. hot water   extra herbs
3 lavender flowers   1 Tbsp. fresh spearmint,
1 c. hot water   for garnish
6 lemons

Combine sweetener and 1 c. of water in a small saucepan over medium heat, stirring until dissolved. Bring to a boil and cook without stirring for 1 minute or until clear. Set aside to cool. Peel the rind of 2 lemons in 1 continuous strip and set aside. Cut all 6 lemons in half. Using a hand juicer, juice all the lemons and strain into a large pitcher. Stir in the cooled syrup and chopped herbs. Add remaining water. Set in the sun or steep for an hour or more. Remove the lemon rind and herbs and chill or serve over ice. Garnish with fresh spearmint and fresh herbs from your garden.

—*Mrs. Leroy B. Miller, Middlefield, OH*

Grape Juice

Pick grapes off stems, wash, put into kettle, and cover with water. Heat to boiling. Pour grapes through a strainer. Put pulp through a food mill and can for pie filling and yogurt. Heat juice to boiling again. Pour into jars and seal. This is a very nice, clear grape juice.

—*Lydia Hostetler, Danville, OH*

It's not just playing – it's growing. They think it's playing when they go romping out in the snow – sliding down the hill, trudging up again. But it's really the way nature makes them work to grow. Sturdy little bodies are built by fresh air, exercise, rest, and nourishing food. See to it that your children have plenty of nourishing food in their diet. This is very important, so that they have plenty of strength and energy.

Rhubarb Drink

1 – 12 oz. frozen orange
  juice concentrate
2 qt. rhubarb concentrate
  (made by using a steam juicer)

3 gal. water
1½-2 c. maple syrup
1 large can pineapple
  juice, optional

Mix all together. Chill and serve.

—*Mary Nolt, Withee, WI*

Easy Punch

1 qt. fresh apple juice
1 qt. cranberry juice

½ c. lemon juice
½ c. honey

Mix juices and chill. Garnish with pineapple chunks if desired.

—*Mary S. Yoder, Wooster, OH*

Vegetable Cocktail

2 c. tomato juice
½ tsp. sea salt
2 Tbsp. lemon juice
1 slice onion
½ c. diced celery

½ c. diced carrots
4 leaves raw spinach
½ tsp. cayenne pepper
4 ice cubes

Blend all ingredients in blender, except ice cubes, until lique-
fied. While blender is running add ice cubes, one at a time, and
allow them to liquefy.

—*Mary S. Yoder, Wooster, OH*

Eggnog

2 eggs, separated
2 c. milk
½ c. maple syrup or honey
¼ tsp. nutmeg

¼ tsp. cinnamon
1 tsp. vanilla
¾ c. whipping cream

Mix egg yolks, milk, maple syrup, spices, and vanilla together. Beat cream and egg whites separately and add to milk mixture. Chill and serve.

—*Mary S. Yoder, Wooster, OH*

Lemonade

6 oz. lemon juice (from real lemons)

4 oz. maple syrup

Mix lemon juice and maple syrup in a 2-qt. pitcher. Fill with water. A very good cleanser.

—*Mrs. Samuel Stoltzfus, Howard, PA*

And said, If thou wilt diligently hearken to the voice of the Lord thy God, and wilt do that which is right in His sight, and wilt give ear to His commandments, and keep all His statutes, I will put none of these diseases upon thee, which I have brought upon the Egyptians: for I am the Lord that healeth thee.
—*Exodus 15:26*

To keep lime deposits out of your teakettles put 2 or 3 marbles in and keep them there.

When you paint and get it on your hands, rub them with vegetable oil or olive oil. Works great with oil base paint.

If your cookies are stuck to the cookie sheet, set the pan on top of the cookstove for a few seconds. It warms them up a bit, making them easy to remove.

Try arrowroot as a thickener. One tablespoon thickens one cup liquid to a medium stage.

When cooking or baking moisten the measuring cup or spoon with oil or water before measuring the honey. This will eliminate sticking.

Are you tired of eating your leftovers in soups and casseroles? If so, try leftover pizza. Simply make your favorite crust, spread with pizza sauce or white sauce (or use leftover gravy) and layer with leftovers. Bake as for pizza.

For best results, pie dough should be worked very lightly after water has been added.

To rid your house from flies, put a sponge in a saucer and saturate with oil of lavender, using one in every room.

Use 1 Tbsp. salt to ¼ c. alcohol to remove grease from clothing by sponging.

Peel onions under water or in draft to prevent "crying".

Salads & Dressings

Health Salad

1 env. unflavored gelatin
1 c. apple juice
1 c. applesauce

1 c. unpeeled apples, cut up
½ c. celery, diced
½ c. nuts, chopped

Mix all together. Chill and serve.

—*Mrs. John Detweiler, Marion, KY*

Apple Cider Salad

2 Tbsp. plain gelatin
3¾ c. apple cider or juice, divided
3 Tbsp. lemon juice
3 Tbsp. honey

¼ tsp. salt, optional
3½-4 c. cored and diced apples
nut meats as desired

Sprinkle gelatin over 1 c. cider in a saucepan. Add honey, lemon, and salt. Heat gently over low heat just until gelatin dissolves. Add remaining cider and pour into a 2-qt. glass bowl. Chill until syrupy. Fold in apples and nut meats. If desired, nuts can be scattered on top instead. Chill until set.

Note: If the apple juice is concentrated, use slightly less water to reconstitute than the can directs.

—*Charlene Kennell, South Wayne, WI*

Apple Salad

2 qt. shredded apples
½ c. raisins
nuts, optional

½ c. cream, whipped
¼ c. peanut butter
⅓ c. maple syrup or honey

Whip the cream. Mix peanut butter with honey or maple syrup and mix with whipped cream. Toss together apples, raisins, and nuts. Add whipped cream and mix till covered.

—*Mary Nolt, Withee, WI*

Potato Salad

12 c. (heaping) cooked,
    chopped potatoes
12 chopped eggs
1½ c. chopped celery
1 c. chopped onion

Dressing:
3 c. homemade mayonnaise
2 Tbsp. mustard
4 tsp. salt
¼ c. vinegar
½ c. honey

Mix dressing ingredients and pour over potato mixture. Add ¼ c. milk if it's too dry.

—Mary Showalter, Mt. Solon, VA

Lebanese Potato Salad

5 lb. potatoes, cooked and
    chopped
½ c. lemon juice
½ c. olive oil

2 tsp. salt
1 c. parsley, chopped
3 cloves garlic, minced
1 onion, chopped

Mix all together.

—Mary Showalter, Mt. Solon, VA

Navy Bean Salad

2 c. dry navy beans
2-3 Tbsp. chopped chives
5 green onions, with tops
    chopped
5 Tbsp. chopped parsley

3 Tbsp. olive oil
2 Tbsp. lemon juice
1 Tbsp. cider vinegar
salt and pepper to taste
1 c. sliced radishes, for garnish

Wash and sort beans. Soak in water overnight. Heat to boiling; reduce heat; simmer until tender or 1½ hour. Cool and drain. Mix all ingredients together except radishes. Marinate overnight. Garnish with radishes.

—Iva Kauffman, Monroe, WI

Taco Salad

1 can kidney beans, rinsed
  and drained
1 lb. Colby cheese, grated
2 medium onions, chopped
10 tomatoes, chopped

2 heads lettuce, chopped
2½ lbs. hamburger
1 pkg. taco seasoning
2 bags tortilla chips, crushed

Brown hamburger and add red pepper, salt, and chili powder to taste. Then add taco seasoning. Cool. Mix other ingredients except tortilla chips. Then add crushed tortilla chips and hamburger just before serving. Serve with your favorite dressing.

—*Mrs. Junior Detweiler, Redding, IA*

Taco Salad

1 large head romaine
  lettuce, cut up
2 large tomatoes, chopped
6 onions, chopped
4 avocados, diced
4 c. brown rice, seasoned with taco seasoning

2 c. kidney beans, cooked
1 c. sliced black olives,
  optional
1 large bag tortilla chips
salsa to taste

Put everything in a large bowl and mix thoroughly.

—*Mrs. John J. Miller, Millersburg, OH*

We remember the fish, which we did eat in Egypt freely; the cucumbers, and the melons, and the leeks, and the onions, and the garlic.

—*Numbers 11:5*

Rainbow Coleslaw

½ head green cabbage, shredded
½ head red cabbage, shredded
1 medium carrot, shredded

Dressing:

⅓ c. milk   1 tsp. honey
½ avocado   ½ tsp. mustard
½ lemon, juiced   ¼ tsp. celery seed
2 tsp. apple cider vinegar   ¼ tsp. sea salt

Put dressing ingredients in blender and blend till creamy. Pour over cabbage.

—*Mrs. John J. Miller, Millersburg, OH*

Fresh Spinach or Dandelion Salad

1 qt. milk   ⅔ c. flour
½ tsp. salt   1 egg
⅔ c. vinegar   3 qt. or more dandelion
⅔ c. maple syrup   or spinach
1 c. milk

Heat 1 quart milk to scalding. Combine salt, vinegar, and maple syrup. Combine the cup of milk, flour, and egg in a separate bowl. Pour vinegar and maple syrup mixture slowly (not too fast) into flour mixture and pour into the scalded milk. Bring to boiling. At first it will have a curdly look, but when it is cooked it will get smooth. Pour over chopped greens and cover with lid. Let stand 10 minutes or until wilted.

—*Mary Nolt, Withee, WI*

Colorful Pepper Salad

3 large green peppers
3 large red peppers
18 cherry tomatoes, halved

3 large yellow peppers,
  thinly sliced

Dressing:
1 Tbsp. mustard
¼ c. red onion, finely chopped
¼ tsp. salt
¼ tsp. garlic powder
3 Tbsp. cider vinegar

¼ tsp. celery seed
3 Tbsp. olive oil
3 Tbsp. honey
⅛ tsp. crushed red
  pepper, optional

Mix dressing all together and pour over salad.

—*Mrs. Leroy B. Miller, Middlefield, OH*

Cucumber Salad

2 qt. cucumbers, shredded
¾ tsp. salt
1½ c. cream

½ c. vinegar
½ c. maple syrup

Mix salt thoroughly with cucumbers. Let stand a few hours or overnight. Drain. Mix vinegar with syrup, then add cream. Pour over cucumbers and mix well.

Note: Always mix vinegar with syrup before adding cream. Cucumbers can also be sliced and packed in bags and put in freezer for winter use.

—*Mary Nolt, Withee, WI*

You can't pick up a heavier load than a grudge.

Broccoli and Cauliflower Salad

1 large head cauliflower
2 bunches broccoli
1 onion, chopped fine
1 c. cheddar cheese, shredded
10-12 pieces bacon, optional

Dressing:
2½ c. Miracle Whip®
2 Tbsp. honey

Separate cauliflower and broccoli into small florets. Mix dressing and pour over all. Refrigerate 24 hours. Add bacon before serving. Yield: 20 servings.

—*Mrs. John Houston, Cottage Grove, TN*

Greens with Herb Dressing

6 Tbsp. olive oil
2 Tbsp. cider or red wine vinegar
2 tsp. mustard
2 tsp. 1 each of 2 of your
    favorite herbs

2 tsp. lemon juice
2 garlic cloves, minced
¼ tsp. salt
dash pepper
8 c. mixed salad greens

Mix together all dressing ingredients and pour over salad greens. Toss and serve.

—*Mrs. Leroy B. Miller, Middlefield, OH*

Vinegar and Oil Salad Dressing

⅓ c. vinegar
1 tsp. salt
½ c. honey
1 tsp. dry mustard

dash of celery seed
¼ c. onion, chopped
1 c. oil

Put all ingredients in blender except oil. Add oil slowly while blending. Keep refrigerated.

—*Loveda Bear, Patriot, OH*

Sesame Oil Salad Dressing

¼ c. cold pressed sesame oil
¼ c. vinegar
¼ c. honey
½ c. avocado

1 c. cottage cheese
1 tsp. cayenne pepper
½ tsp. sea salt
¼ clove garlic, minced

Mix in blender until smooth.

—Mary S. Yoder, Wooster, OH

Poppy Seed Dressing

½ c. honey
1 tsp. dry mustard
⅓ c. vinegar

1 c. olive oil
1 Tbsp. poppy seeds

Mix together in blender. Stir in poppy seeds. Serve over lettuce salad or tossed salad.

—Mary Showalter, Mt. Solon, VA

Dressing for Cabbage or Lettuce

1 tsp. maple syrup
1 tsp. lemon juice

1 tsp. vinegar
1 tsp. olive oil, optional

Yield: 1 serving. Adjust to suit your needs.

—Elizabeth Drudge, Wroxeter, Ontario

For one believeth that he may eat all things:
another, who is weak, eateth herbs.
—Romans 14:2

Western Dressing

2 c. mayonnaise or healthy
   alternative
¾ c. honey

¼ c. vinegar
½ c. ketchup

Mix all together and serve over salads.

—*Mrs. Elmer Esh, Burkesville, KY*

Blue Cheese Dressing

½ c. sour cream
2 c. salad dressing
¼ c. vinegar

2 Tbsp. honey
1 c. blue cheese, crumbled

Beat all ingredients except cheese. Add cheese and mix well.

—*Mary S. Yoder, Wooster, OH*

Dressing for Potato Salad

2 Tbsp. rounded spelt flour
½ tsp. salt
¼ tsp. stevia
½ tsp. dry mustard

1 egg, beaten
2 Tbsp. oil
¾ c. water
¼ c. vinegar or lemon juice

Combine dry ingredients in saucepan. Turn heat to medium.
Beat together other ingredients and add slowly to dry ingredients
while stirring. Heat and stir till thick and bubbly. Cool.

—*Laura Yoder, Free Union, VA*

Simple Salad Dressing

1 c. plain yogurt
¼ c. olive oil
3 Tbsp. vinegar

3 Tbsp. maple syrup
1 tsp. salt

Blend well. Add to chopped vegetables just before eating.

—Mrs. Joe Garber, Prattsburgh, NY

Homemade Garlic Mayonnaise

1 egg yolk
½ tsp. prepared mustard
salt to taste

2 garlic cloves, minced
¾ c. oil
2 Tbsp. lemon juice

Combine egg yolk, mustard, salt, and garlic. Whisk together. Gradually add the oil. Once blended, add lemon juice. Keep refrigerated.

—Mrs. Leroy B. Miller, Middlefield, OH

Mayonnaise

1 egg, plus enough water to
   make ½ c.
¾ c. olive oil
1 tsp. dry mustard
⅓ c. honey

2 tsp. salt
1 Tbsp. lemon juice
⅓ c. tapioca starch
½ c. vinegar
1¼ c. hot water

Beat egg, water, oil, mustard, honey, salt, and lemon juice together thoroughly with beater. Mix starch with vinegar; add to water and cook in heavy saucepan. Bring to a boil, then mix with beaten mixture. Beat hard until smooth.

—Mary Fisher, Rebersburg, PA

Mayonnaise

1 very fresh egg
¾ tsp. salt
½ tsp. dry mustard
¼ tsp. paprika, optional

1 Tbsp. vinegar
1 Tbsp. lemon juice
1 c. olive oil

In blender, blend all but oil. Slowly add oil while blending. Yield: about 1¼ c.

—Mary Showalter, Mt. Solon, VA

Miracle Whip®

1¾ c. water
½ c. vinegar
⅔ c. flour
1 egg
¾ c. butter, softened

2 Tbsp. honey
2 Tbsp. maple syrup
2 tsp. salt
1 tsp. lemon juice
1 tsp. mustard

Cook water, vinegar, and flour until thick. Process the rest of ingredients in blender on high till creamy. Add cooked mixture and blend on high till creamy.

—Mrs. John Houston, Cottage Grove, TN

Sweet and Sour Dressing

6 oz. olive oil
3 oz. apple cider vinegar

¼-½ c. honey

Mix well in a shaker jar, then pour on salad.

—Mrs. John J. Miller, Millersburg, OH

Family French Dressing

1 c. ketchup	⅓ c. honey
1 c. olive oil	1 tsp. paprika
⅓ c. cider vinegar	1 tsp. salt or to taste
1 Tbsp. lemon juice	wedge of onion

Place all ingredients in blender and blend well. Serve with tossed salads.

—*Charlene Kennell, South Wayne, WI*

French Dressing

1 tsp. lemon juice	¼ tsp. salt
4 Tbsp. oil, divided	¼ tsp. paprika
¼ tsp. honey	

Mix together dry ingredients and 1¼ Tbsp. of the oil. Stir well and add lemon juice and honey. As dressing thickens through stirring, add the rest of oil and a little garlic flavor if you like.

—*Mrs. John Detweiler, Marion, KY*

Recommendations of major dietary changes, with wasteful neglect of nutritious food, such as butter, eggs, whole milk, cheeses, and beef, border on irresponsibility and smacks of medical quackery.
—K. A. Oster, 1974

Soups

Harvest Home Soup

1 lb. combination of:
  yellow split peas
  green split peas
  red lentils and lentils
  brown rice and wild rice
8 c. water
1 lb. cooked ground beef, chicken, or turkey

2 c. carrots, sliced
2 c. celery, sliced
2 c. cabbage, optional
1½-2 qt. whole tomatoes
  or tomato juice

Add peas, lentils, and/or rice to water and simmer for 1 hour. Add rest of ingredients. Simmer 1 hour. Season to taste.

—*Charlene Kennell, South Wayne, WI*

Chili Soup

2 lb. hamburger
2 onions, chopped
1 Tbsp. salt, divided
2 qt. tomato juice
1 pt. dark kidney beans

2 tsp. chili powder
⅛ tsp. oregano
⅛ tsp. basil
⅛ tsp. rosemary
⅛ tsp. stevia

Brown hamburger, onions, and 2 tsp. salt. In a large kettle combine the rest of ingredients, including 1 tsp. salt. Add browned hamburger mixture. Simmer all afternoon for best flavor.

—*Mrs. John Houston, Cottage Grove, TN*

To live as gently as I can;
To be, no matter what, a man;
To take what comes of good or ill,
And cling to faith and honor still.
    —*Edgar Guest*

Hearty Hamburger Soup

1 lb. ground beef
2 onions, chopped
1 tsp. salt
2 c. tomato juice
1 c. carrots, diced
1 c. potatoes, diced

½ c. chopped celery
1½ tsp. salt
dash of pepper
⅓ c. flour
4 c. milk, divided

Brown ground beef, onions, and salt in a large kettle. Add next 6 ingredients. Stir together flour and 1 c. milk and add to soup. Simmer 20-25 minutes. Add the remaining 3 c. milk before serving.

—*Mrs. John Houston, Cottage Grove, TN*

Split Pea Soup with Ham

2 ham hocks or large ham bone
2 large onions, chopped
2 celery stalks, chopped

1 lb. dry split peas
1 tsp. salt
⅛ tsp. pepper

Simmer meat in 2 qt. water for 30 minutes. Add split peas and cook slowly for an additional 1½ hours. Cut meat into pieces and return to soup. Add celery and onion. Cook ½ hour more or until veggies are tender. Add salt and pepper to taste. You may have to add more water. Yield: 10 c.

—*Mrs. Leroy B. Miller, Middlefield, OH*

Confess your faults one to another, and pray for each other that ye may be healed. The effectual fervent prayer of a righteous man availeth much.
—*James 5:16*

Velvety Chicken Soup

1 c. brown rice	1 c. milk
3 c. water	3 c. chicken broth
½ c. butter	2 c. chicken, diced
1 onion, chopped	8 oz. cream of mushroom soup
½ c. whole grain flour or arrowroot powder	

Cook rice in water. In another kettle, sauté onion in butter. Add flour, then milk. When thick add chicken broth, diced chicken, and mushroom soup. Add rice and simmer 20 minutes or so.

—*Mrs. John Houston, Cottage Grove, TN*

Cream of Chicken Soup

½ c. butter	2 c. chicken broth
1 onion, chopped	3 Tbsp. chicken base
1½ c. whole grain flour	(without MSG)
1 c. milk	1 Tbsp. salt

Melt butter; add onion and flour. Stir well. Add milk, chicken broth, soup base, and salt. Cook until thick. Use in recipes calling for cream of chicken soup.

You can also can this by spooning into pint jars and cold packing 20 minutes. You can also freeze it.

Variations: Cream of mushroom soup – 2 c. chopped mushrooms
Cream of celery soup – 2 c. chopped celery
Cream of onion – 2 c. chopped onion

—*Mrs. John Houston, Cottage Grove, TN*

> *A merry heart doeth good like a medicine: but a broken spirit*
> *drieth the bones.*
> —*Proverbs 17:22*

Vegetable Soup

1 lb. hamburger	¼ tsp. rosemary
1 tsp. salt	¼ tsp. oregano
2 onions, chopped	½ tsp. chili powder
2 c. carrots, chopped	1 tsp. salt
2 c. potatoes, diced	2 c. tomato juice
1 c. celery, chopped	2 c. peas
½ tsp. basil	

Brown hamburger, onions, and salt. In a large kettle, cook together carrots, potatoes, and celery. Add browned meat, herbs, seasonings, and tomato juice. Simmer 30-60 minutes. Just before serving add the peas.

—*Mrs. John Houston, Cottage Grove, TN*

Ham and Bean Soup

1 lb. ham	1½ c. potatoes, cubed
1 lb. navy beans	salt and pepper to taste
1½ c. tomato juice	

Soak navy beans overnight, then cook until soft. Cook ham and potatoes until soft, then mix together all ingredients. Add water to desired consistency. Heat to boiling before serving.

—*Mrs. Edward Martin, Alta Vista, IA*

Making mistakes isn't dumb; disregarding them is.

Bean Soup

1 large onion, chopped	1 tsp. thyme
3 medium carrots, diced	2 bay leaves
2 garlic cloves, crushed	1½ Tbsp. parsley flakes
2 c. dried beans*	salt and pepper
8 c. boiling water	2 c. tomatoes

Soak beans overnight, then add to boiling water along with all other ingredients except tomatoes. Bring to boil and simmer until beans and vegetables are soft. Add tomatoes and bring to boil. Remove bay leaves before serving.

*Any kind of beans can be used. We prefer mixed beans.

—*Mrs. Edward Martin, Alta Vista, IA*

Chicken Noodle Soup

1½ lb. whole wheat noodles	¾ c. carrots, chopped
2 pt. chicken pieces, canned	1 small onion, chopped
1 pt. chicken broth	½-¾ c. chicken-style seasoning
¾ c. celery, chopped	vege salt to taste, optional

Sauté veggies in broth in 8-qt. saucepan. Once tender add water to fill about ½ full. Bring to a boil; add noodles, chicken, and seasonings. Cook until noodles are tender. Add more water if necessary.

—*Sharon Troyer, Millersburg, OH*

The Kellogg report: As peculiar contemporary illnesses, they are caused by affluent overloads of once rare substances, from nicotine to sugar to cocaine, that now flood our society.

Cream of Potato Soup

6 medium potatoes, scrubbed, shredded, and cubed

¾ c. celery	1 c. soaked almonds
2 large carrots, shredded	2 c. water
1 onion, chopped	½ c. whole wheat flour
1 tsp. vege salt	¼-½ c. chicken-style seasoning (more or less to taste)

Cover veggies with water and salt, and cook until tender. Blend almonds (that have been soaked in water for 12 hours) with 1 c. of water till creamy, then slowly add another c. of water. Blend well. Add chicken seasoning and flour. Add this mixture to soup. Heat. May add broccoli or peas while heating the second time to vary flavors. For a less thick soup omit flour.

—*Mrs. Joni Troyer, Millersburg, OH*

Cream of Potato Soup

2 c. raw potatoes, grated	2 c. milk
1½ c. water	⅛ tsp. garlic salt
¾ tsp. salt	¼ tsp. celery flakes
2 eggs	

Cook together potatoes, water, and salt for 5-10 minutes, stirring often. Stir in the eggs. Then add the milk and seasonings.

—*Mary Fisher, Rebersburg, PA*

The rich ruleth over the poor, and the borrower is servant to the lender.
—Proverbs 22:7

Lima Bean Soup

2 c. dried lima beans	2 c. tomatoes
1 c. celery, chopped	½ c. oil
1 c. carrots, cubed	3 Tbsp. parsley
3 onions, chopped	½ tsp. sage

Soak beans in water overnight. In the morning, add the rest of ingredients and cook at a simmer until tender.

—*Mrs. Leroy Auker, Elk Horn, KY*

Chicken Noodle Soup

½ c. carrots, diced	1 tsp. salt
¼ c. celery, diced	½ tsp. dried marjoram
¼ c. onion, chopped	½ tsp. dried thyme
2 tsp. butter	⅛ tsp. pepper
6 c. chicken broth	1½ c. uncooked noodles
1½ c. cooked chicken, diced	1 Tbsp. fresh parsley, minced

Sauté carrots, celery, and onion in butter until tender. Add broth, chicken, and seasonings; bring to a boil. Reduce heat. Add noodles. Cook 10 minutes or until tender. Add parsley. Water and chicken seasoning may be used instead of broth. Yield: 6 servings.

—*Pauline Schrock, Clayton, IL*

Even a fool, when he holdeth his peace, is counted wise: and he that shutteth his lips is esteemed a man of understanding.
—*Proverbs 17:28*

Beefy Garden Soup

1 lb. ground beef
1 small onion, chopped
¼ c. celery, chopped
6 potatoes, diced
¼ head cabbage, cut into
  bite-size pieces

1 qt. chopped tomatoes or
  tomato juice
½ pt. fresh or frozen corn
  with liquid
salt and pepper to taste

Brown ground beef and onion until well done. Drain. Combine ground beef/onion mixture and remaining ingredients in large pot, adding extra water to cover vegetables. (A cup of beef broth may be used for part of the water if desired.) Bring to a boil, then lower to simmer, stirring occasionally. Cook until vegetables are tender.

—*Mary E. Showalter, Mt. Solon, VA*

Chicken, Corn, and Rice Soup

1 qt. cooked chicken, diced
1 qt. chicken broth
1 medium onion
½ c. celery or celery leaves,
  chopped
1 qt. corn, fresh or frozen

1½ c. brown rice
1 qt. water
1 Tbsp. salt
pepper to taste
¼ c. parsley, chopped,
  optional

Cook together until tender. Serve.

—*Mary E. Showalter, Mt. Solon, VA*

Forgiveness is not an occasional act; it is a permanent attitude.

Broccoli Soup

1 head broccoli, cut in large pieces
3 c. water   ¼ c. butter
2 oz. carrots, shredded   10 Tbsp. flour
¼ c. celery, chopped   5 c. hot milk
¼ c. ham, chopped   4 oz. cheese, grated
⅓ c. onion, chopped   1 Tbsp. chicken soup base

Bring the broccoli to a boil in 3 cups water; reduce heat and simmer 1-2 minutes. Drain and save water. Add chicken base to broccoli water. Chop drained broccoli until mushy. In the meantime, cook carrots and celery together until tender. Fry ham and onions in butter; add flour to form a sauce. Add to hot milk. Now add broccoli, broccoli water, and cooked vegetables to hot milk mixture. Add cheese before serving.

—*Gertie Troyer, Loganville, WI*

Trust in the Lord with all thine heart: and lean not unto thine own understanding. In all thy ways acknowledge Him, and He shall direct thy paths. Be not wise in thine own eyes; fear the Lord, and depart from evil. It shall be health to thy navel, and strength to thy bones.
—*Proverbs 3:5-8*

Gravies & Sauces

Liver and Onion Gravy

1 lb. liver, sliced thin (beef or chicken)
2 Tbsp. fat   1 tsp. salt
1 onion   ⅛ tsp. pepper
2 Tbsp. flour   water

Melt fat; add minced onion and cook until light brown. Add thinly sliced liver pieces. Stir frequently until liver is browned. Add flour and let it brown. Add water until desired consistency is obtained. Season. Cook until gravy is thickened.

—*Mrs. Edward Martin, Alta Vista, IA*

Hamburger Pan Gravy

⅓ c. butter   5½ c. milk
½ c. onions, chopped   1½ tsp. salt
½ c. hamburger, crumbled   dash pepper
1 c. whole wheat flour

In a heavy saucepan or iron skillet, melt the butter and add onions. Sauté the onions then add meat. Fry for one minute; add flour and stir well with spatula. Brown for half a minute then add milk, ½-1 c. at a time, stirring well after each addition. After milk has all been added and gravy is smooth, let it boil several seconds. Take off heat and add salt and pepper. Serve over pancakes, biscuits, or potatoes.

—*Miss Miriam Yutzy, Howe, IN*

Be not deceived; God is not mocked: for whatsoever a man soweth, that shall he also reap.
—*Galations 6:7*

Chicken Pan Gravy

¼ c. oil	2½ pt. milk
¾ c. whole wheat flour	2 tsp. salt

After you are done frying chicken, make this gravy in the same pan with the drippings and all. Make sure you have ¼ c. oil in the pan. Add the flour all at once and stir with a spatula. Brown for about half a minute, stirring it constantly. Add milk, ½-1 c. at a time, stirring well after each addition. After milk has all been added and gravy is smooth, let it boil several seconds. Remove from heat and add salt. Serve over potatoes or with chicken.

—*Mrs. Raymond Yutzy, Howe, IN*

Tomato Gravy

6 c. milk, divided	1½ c. whole wheat flour
1½ c. tomato juice	2 tsp. salt

Heat, but do not boil, 3 c. milk and tomato juice. Make a paste with the remaining 3 c. milk and flour and add to hot tomato mixture. Stir well and keep on stirring as it thickens. Bring to a boil and boil several seconds. Add salt and serve. Can be served with biscuits, corn bread, fried mush, zucchini patties, eggplant, etc.

—*Miss Mary Beth Yutzy, Howe, IN*

Pleasant words are as an honeycomb, sweet to the soul and health to the bones.
—*Proverbs 16:24*

73

Chicken Gravy

¼ c. butter	3 c. milk
¼ c. celery, chopped	1¼ c. whole wheat flour
¼ c. onions, chopped	2 tsp. salt
½ c. carrots, shredded	dash pepper
1 c. potatoes, shredded	½ tsp. tumeric
1 qt. chicken broth	

In a heavy 3-qt. saucepan, melt the butter and add all the vegetables. Cover and cook over low heat until vegetables are tender. Add chicken broth and bring to a boil. Make a paste with the milk and flour and add to boiling mixture. Stir and bring to a boil over medium heat. Boil several seconds. Add salt and pepper or seasonings of your choice. Serve over biscuits.

Note: You may want to can the vegetables together, then you can omit the butter and start by just heating 1 pt. vegetables with the broth.

—*Mrs. Raymond Yutzy, Howe, IN*

Cheese Sauce

1 c. butter	3 c. milk or cream
3 Tbsp. onions, chopped	salt to taste
7 Tbsp. whole wheat flour	5 lb. cheese, shredded or cubed
1 c. water	milk

Melt butter in an 8-qt. kettle. Add onions and sauté over low heat. Add flour and stir over low heat for 3-4 minutes. Add water, stirring rapidly with a fork or wire whip until smooth. Add milk or cream and cheese, stirring over medium heat until well blended. Add more milk until it reaches desired consistency. Heat, and salt to taste.

—*Mrs. Vernon Hershberger, Loganville, WI*

White Sauce

⅓ c. butter	1 pt. milk
⅓ c. onions, chopped fine	1 tsp. salt
⅓ c. whole wheat flour	

In a medium-sized heavy saucepan, melt butter and add onions. Fry for several minutes on medium heat. Add flour and brown for 1 minute. Add milk, ½ c. at a time, stirring well after each addition. Add salt. Boil several seconds.

Variation: For cheese sauce add ½ c. more milk and ½-¾ c. cheese. This is very good on vegetables or casseroles.

—*Mrs. Raymond Yutzy, Howe, IN*

Honey Barbecue Sauce

½ c. onion, chopped	½ tsp. salt
2 garlic cloves, minced	1 tsp. prepared mustard
1½ c. ketchup	½ tsp. black pepper
2 Tbsp. vinegar	1 c. honey

Mix all ingredients and cook over low heat for 3-4 minutes. Use on beef, pork, or chicken.

—*Mrs. Daniel Otto, Topeka, IN*

Sauce for Grilling Meat

1 c. melted butter or olive oil	1 tsp. paprika
2 tsp. garlic salt	

Brush on meat while grilling.

—*Mrs. Mervin H. Yoder, Pleasant Hill, IL*

Barbecue Sauce

1½ c. catsup   1 onion, chopped
¼ c. vinegar   1 tsp. salt
¼ c. sorghum   1 c. water or broth, optional

Pour over lamb, beef, or chicken and cook until meat is tender.

—*Mary Showalter, Mt. Solon, VA*

Be still, my soul, and listen,
For God would speak to thee,
And while the tempest's raging
Thy refuge He would be.

Be still, and cease to struggle,
Seek not to understand;
The flames will not destroy thee,
Thou'rt in the Father's hand.

And when the burden's heavy
He seeks to make thee pure,
To give thee faith and patience
And courage to endure.

The way is not too hard for thee,
Endure the chastening rod;
Thy gold shall only be refined,
Be still, submit to God.
—G. W. S.

Meats & Vegetables

Wholesome Meats and Fats

Let us take a short look at confinement-raised versus meat from animals who are allowed to graze and live in a natural environment.

For thousands of years our ancestors thrived on animal foods from cows, goats, sheep, and wild game which were foraging and grazing on the natural vegetation of the land. Meat, cultured milk, butter, and cheese, along with eggs, fruits, vegetables, grains, and olive oil were their main foods. Modern diseases were almost nonexistent.

Today there is a significant difference in the way our commercial meats are raised. Huge, factory-type barns and feedlots are packed with thousands of animals. Commercial feeds contain many waste products, antibiotics, hormones, and grain that has been sprayed with toxic weed killer, fungicide, and insecticides.

It is easy to see that to raise animals in fresh air and sunshine, letting them feed on green grass, insects, organic minerals, and limited amounts of organic grains is a much healthier way. Farming with this natural method produces nutrient-dense meat, eggs, milk, cheese, yogurt, and especially butter. These wholesome nutritious foods are very rich in vitamins, minerals, and essential fatty acids.

Omega-3 is an essential fatty acid (which means our bodies cannot make them). Every cell and system in our bodies, including the brain, need omega-3s. Grass-fed meat, milk, and eggs have 3-5 times more of omega-3 than the factory-grown meat, milk, and eggs.

CLA is another very important fatty acid. The richest source known is meat, milk, and butter from ruminating animals grazing on green grass. (CLA is made in the rumen.) Butterfat contains a very high CLA content. Nonfat milk products contain hardly any CLA.

Adequate amounts of omega-3 and CLA can help prevent many diseases including cancer, heart disease, diabetes, and mental disorders.

Butter made from cream is also a good source of Vitamins A, D, E, and K and trace minerals. With all these vitamins and minerals, along with being a good source of omega-3 and CLA, butter is our number one choice of fats.

Olive oil has been used since Bible times with super health results. Use extra-virgin olive oil at moderate temperatures and not as your only fat. Our bodies need nutrients that are found only in animal fats.

If you have diabetes or hypoglycemia, you may need more good fat in your diet to keep blood sugar levels stable. Eating good, natural fats does not make you fat. The human brain is over 60% fat, our hormones are made from fat, the outer layer of every cell in our bodies is fat. Natural, unprocessed, unhydrogenated fat helps our heart, skin, and immune system.

Some of the most harmful fats used are the popular vegetable oils – soy, corn, cottonseed, canola, sunflower, and safflower. To produce these fragile, unbalanced oils, the seeds are processed with high temperatures and toxic chemical solvents. This process destroys many of the natural vitamins and antioxidants, causing the oil to become rancid. Rancid oils produce free radicals which are responsible for many diseases.

Margarine and shortening have been called the plastic fats because of being partially hydrogenated. This is a complicated process which involves the mixing of oils with tiny metal particles, hydrogen gas, thickening agents, bleaching, coloring, and flavoring. This high-temperature process causes the fatty acid molecules to rearrange themselves into transfats, a formation not commonly found in nature.

These toxic fats are difficult to digest and defective to our bodies, clogging up our blood vessels with a toxic sludge. If our diets are deficient in good fats which we need, our bodies substitute some of the defective fats and we become partially hydrogenated.

Many of our vital systems become defective when we substitute unnatural fats for normal healthy fats. This leads to lowered immunity and less resistance to many diseases.

Sloppy Joes

1 lb. ground beef
½ c. onion, chopped
½ c. green pepper
8 oz. tomatoes, chopped

2 Tbsp. quick oats
1-1½ tsp. chili seasoning
½ tsp. garlic salt
¼ c. water

Brown meat, onions, and peppers. Drain. Stir in remaining ingredients. Bring to a boil; reduce heat and simmer for 5-10 minutes or till desired consistency.

—*Miriam Yoder, Baltic, OH*

Meat Loaf

1½ lb. ground beef
¾ c. uncooked oatmeal
2 eggs, beaten
¼ c. onions

2 tsp. salt
¼ tsp. pepper
1 c. tomato juice

Combine all ingredients and press in pan. Bake at 350° for 1 hour.

—*Miss Betty Hilty, Oakfield, ME*

Saucy Meatloaf

1 egg, slightly beaten
2 Tbsp. ketchup
1¾ tsp. salt
¾ tsp. chili powder
dash of pepper
¼ c. onion, chopped
½ c. milk

1 c. quick oats
1½ lb. ground meat

Topping:
¼ c. ketchup
½ Tbsp. honey
½ tsp. mustard

Bake at 350° for 45 minutes. Add topping. Bake for 15 more minutes.

—*Mrs. Mervin H. Yoder, Pleasant Hill, IL*

Barbecued Meatballs

3 lb. ground beef
1½ c. milk
2 c. dry fine bread crumbs
2 eggs
½ c. dry onion

½ tsp. garlic powder
2 tsp. salt
½ tsp. pepper
2 tsp. chili powder

Mix all together and shape into balls. Arrange in cake pans. Mix and pour following sauce over meatballs. Bake uncovered at 350° for 1 hour.

Sauce:
2½ c. ketchup
¼ c. mustard
½ tsp. garlic powder

¼ tsp. salt
¼ c. onion, chopped

—Mrs. Raymond Yutzy, Howe, IN

Mock Steak

3 lb. hamburger
1 c. water
1 c. fine dry bread crumbs

2 tsp. salt
¼ tsp. pepper

Mix together well; put in covered pan to chill overnight. Slice, roll in flour, and fry. Place in layers in roaster and cover with hamburger pan gravy. Bake at 325° for 1 hour. Shredded cheese may be added after each layer of meat.

—Mrs. Raymond Yutzy, Howe, IN

These are the beasts which ye shall eat: the ox, the sheep, the goat,...and the deer. These ye shall eat of all that are in the waters: all that have fins and scales shall ye eat...of all clean birds ye shall eat.

—*Deuteronomy 14:4-5, 9,11*

Vegetable Meat Loaf

2 lb. hamburger
1 c. raw beets, grated
1 c. raw carrots, grated
1 onion, chopped
2 eggs

¾ c. ketchup
1 c. whole wheat bread
  crumbs
1½ tsp. salt
pepper

Mix. Bake at 350° for 1 hour.

—Iva Kauffman, Monroe, WI

Carrot Nut Loaf

2 c. carrots, coarsely chopped
½ c. bread crumbs, toasted
1 c. celery, chopped
¾ c. walnuts, chopped

1 c. tomatoes, mashed
½ c. onions, sliced and
  braised
2 Tbsp. butter

Mix first 6 ingredients together; add butter. Place in a loaf pan and bake ½ hour at 350°.

—Mrs. John Detweiler, Marion, KY

Beef Stew

3 c. potatoes, diced
1 c. carrots, diced
¼ c. onion, diced
2 c. beef or broth

salt and pepper
2 Tbsp. cornstarch
2 c. canned peas

Boil potatoes, carrots, and onions till tender. Add beef or broth and cover with water. Season with salt and pepper. When boiling mix cornstarch with a little water and add. Last add peas. Bring to a boil. Serve.

—Amelia Troyer, Glenford, OH

Ham and Thin Noodles

1 pkg. whole grain thin noodles
2-4 garlic cloves, minced
¼ c. olive oil

⅓ c. Parmesan cheese
½ lb. fully cooked ham, cubed
¼ c. fresh parsley, minced

Cook pasta. Meanwhile, in a skillet sauté garlic in oil for 1 minute. Stir in cubed ham and heat through, about 2 minutes. Drain pasta and toss with ham mixture. Sprinkle with cheese and parsley.

Note: If you don't have ham try substituting crumbled bacon or use both.

—*Mrs. Leroy B. Miller, Middlefield, OH*

Tasty Roast Chicken

1 chicken, cut up
1 c. cornmeal
1 tsp. salt
1 tsp. paprika

1 tsp. ground mustard
pepper, optional
sweet basil flakes, dried
  and crushed

Mix the cornmeal and seasonings. Roll the chicken in the cornmeal mixture and place in baking pan. Sprinkle with sweet basil leaves. Dot with homemade butter. Bake at 375° until tender.

—*Mrs. Simon Borntrager, Beeville, TX*

The fear of the Lord is the beginning of wisdom; and the knowledge of the holy is understanding.
—*Proverbs 9:10*

Baked Chicken Cutlets

6 boneless, skinless chicken
 breasts
1¼ c. Italian-style dry bread
 crumbs
½ c. Parmesan cheese
2 Tbsp. wheat germ

1 Tbsp. flaxseed
1 Tbsp. sesame seeds
1 tsp. dried basil
½ tsp. garlic powder
1 c. plain yogurt

Flatten chicken to ½" thickness. Combine crumbs, cheese, wheat germ, flaxseed, sesame seeds, basil, and garlic powder. Put yogurt in another bowl. Dip chicken in yogurt then coat with crumb mixture. Put on oiled cookie sheet. Spritz with oil or melted butter. Bake uncovered for 20-25 minutes at 350°.

—*Mrs. Leroy B. Miller, Middlefield, OH*

Honeyed Chicken

1 chicken, cut up
¼ c. butter, melted
½ c. honey

¼ c. mustard
1 tsp. garlic salt
1 tsp. curry powder

Place chicken in baking dish. Mix rest of ingredients together and pour over chicken. Bake at 350° for 1½ hours, turning every 15 minutes.

—*Mary Detweiler, West Farmington, OH*

For whom the Lord loveth He correcteth; even as a father the
son in whom he delighteth.
—*Proverbs 3:12*

Crunchy Chicken

4 c. cooked chicken, cut into
   bite-size pieces
½ c. melted butter
¾ c. bread crumbs

½ c. Colby cheese, shredded
dash of pepper
½ tsp. salt

Mix all ingredients together. Place on a cookie sheet that is covered with lightly greased tinfoil. Bake at 400° for 10 minutes.

—*Erma Hoover, Penn Yan, NY*

Baked Chicken

Cut 1 fryer up; soak in salt water overnight. Drain well. Dip in melted butter, then crushed crackers. Place skin side up on broiler pan. Bake at 400° for 10 minutes. Reduce heat to 350° for 50 minutes or until tender.

—*Mrs. Junior Detweiler, Redding, IA*

Baked Fish Fillets

Grease pan. Place fillets in single layer and spread with salad dressing. Sprinkle generously with wheat germ. Top with preferred seasoning. Bake at 350° until fish flakes easily. This tastes like it's fried, but it is much better for you.

—*Mrs. Mervin H. Yoder, Pleasant Hill, IL*

He who seldom thinks of Heaven is not likely to get there.

Baked Fish Fillets

Arrange fresh or thawed fish in baking pan. Dot with butter (optional). Sprinkle with lemon pepper or pepper and garlic salt. Bake at 350° until fish flakes easily.

—*Mrs. Mervin H. Yoder, Pleasant Hill, IL*

Fish Cakes

1 c. flaked fish (salmon or flounder)
2 Tbsp. butter or oil, divided
1 small onion, chopped

1 egg
⅓ c. whole grain bread crumbs
1 tsp. fresh dill or seeds, chopped

In large skillet, sauté onions in half of butter. Combine with rest of ingredients. Form into cakes. Pan broil in remaining butter or oil until golden brown. Garnish with parsley.

—*Mrs. Leroy Auker, Elk Horn, KY*

Tuna Patties

2 (7 oz.) cans tuna, drained
1 c. dry bread crumbs

2 eggs, beaten
¼ c. onion, minced

Mix lightly; shape into patties and fry. Serve on lettuce and tomatoes. Can also be baked.

—*Mrs. Junior Detweiler, Redding, IA*

The sleep of a laboring man is sweet, whether he eat little or much: but the abundance of the rich will not suffer him to sleep.

Ecclesiastes 5:12

Vegetable Sunburgers

½ c. carrots, grated	1 Tbsp. oil
½ c. celery, finely chopped	¼ c. tomato juice
2 Tbsp. onion, chopped	1 c. ground sunflower seed
1 Tbsp. green pepper, chopped	2 Tbsp. wheat germ
1 Tbsp. parsley, chopped	⅛ tsp. dried basil
1 egg, beaten	

Preheat oven to 350°. Combine all ingredients and shape into patties. Arrange in an oiled shallow baking pan. Bake until brown on top, then turn over. Bake 15 minutes again.

—*Mrs. Leroy Auker, Elk Horn, KY*

Speedy Black Bean Burritos

1 (15 oz.) can black beans, drained	1 tomato, diced
¼ c. salsa	4 flour tortillas
3 Tbsp. uncooked bulgur wheat	1 c. leaf lettuce, shredded

Combine beans, salsa, and wheat in a saucepan and simmer 5 minutes. Remove from heat and cover. Shred lettuce and dice the tomato. Heat tortillas in an ungreased skillet. Spread a line of bean mixture down the center of a burrito; top with lettuce, tomato, and additional salsa. Roll tortilla around filling. Serve.

—*Mrs. Leroy B. Miller, Middlefield, OH*

Tender Hamburgers

1½ lb. hamburger	¼ tsp. pepper
½ c. fine dry bread crumbs	½ c. milk or tomato juice
¼ c. onions, chopped	1 egg
1½ tsp. salt	

Mix all together. Shape into patties. Roll in flour and fry.

—*Michael Yutzy, Howe, IN*

Chicken Fritters

4 c. chicken, finely diced	4 eggs
½ c. mushrooms, optional	½ c. celery, chopped
4 c. mashed potatoes	1 onion, chopped

Cook onion and celery till soft. Mix all together. Add milk to moisten. Fry in hot oil.

—*Iva Kauffman, Monroe, WI*

Mock Chicken Croquettes

2 parts onion, braised	1 part carrots
2 parts green bell pepper	1 part peas
2 parts celery	whole wheat bread crumbs
1 part potatoes	oil

Simmer vegetables until soft. Mix all together and mash fine. Add whole wheat bread crumbs to make thick enough to handle. Mold into croquettes and bake in oil until a nice golden brown. May also be mixed together in evening and finished the next day.

—*Mrs. Abie J. Troyer, Ashland, OH*

Homemade Gyros

Wrap flour tortillas in foil and heat in 350° oven for 15-20 minutes or until warm. Fry ham or homemade bologna in lightly oiled skillet. Spread salad dressing on warm tortillas; add ham or bologna, cheese, mustard, sliced onions, lettuce, sprouts, or whatever toppings you prefer. Roll up and serve like sandwiches.

—*Mrs. Mervin Yoder, Pleasant Hill, IL*

Chili Verde (Green Chili Enchiladas)

10 -12 flour tortillas

Sauce:
¼ c. olive oil
1 small onion, chopped
2 large garlic cloves, chopped
½ tsp. ground cumin
½ tsp. black pepper

1 lb. Montery Jack cheese, shredded

3 c. chicken broth
2 (4 oz.) cans green chilies, diced
½ tsp. oregano
1 tsp. salt
2-3 Tbsp. flour

Heat oil in a 1-2 qt. saucepan over medium heat. Add onion and garlic; cover and cook on low for 5 minutes. Raise heat to medium, stir in flour, cumin, and black pepper, and cook stirring, 2 minutes. Remove from heat and gradually pour in broth (whisk to remove lumps). Add remaining ingredients and bring to a boil. Cook on low and simmer 30 minutes. The finished mixture should be fairly thick. Drench tortillas in this mixture and fill with refried beans (or chicken) and cheese. Roll and place in baking dish side by side. Cover with remaining sauce and cheese. Cover ends to keep from drying. Bake at 350° for 15 minutes.

—*Bertha Peachey, Hamptonville, NC*

Pita Sandwiches

Shape bread dough into oval bun-sized rolls. Put on greased cookie sheet and let rise 10-15 minutes. Bake at 350° for 20 minutes or until done. Cool. Cut them partly open at the side, enough to form a pocket. Stuff pocket with any mixture or salad fixings and dressing.

Variation: For hot sandwiches use chicken or tuna salad, pizza toppings, or ham and cheese.

—*Mrs. Mervin Yoder, Pleasant Hill, IL*

Chicken and Turkey Rollup

2½ c. chicken breast or
   turkey baked and cubed
1½ c. sour cream
1 Tbsp. taco seasoning
1½ c. cream of mushroom soup
2 c. cheese, shredded

1 small onion, chopped
½ c. salsa
10 flour tortillas
shredded lettuce
chopped tomatoes

In a bowl, combine chicken or turkey and ½ c. sour cream, ½ tsp. taco seasoning, ½ c. soup, 1 c. cheese, onion, and salsa. Place ½ c. of this mixture on each tortilla. Roll up and place seams down on a greased cookie sheet. Combine remaining sour cream, taco seasoning, and soup. Pour over tortillas. Cover and bake at 350° for 30 minutes or until well heated. Sprinkle with remaining cheese.

Note: Warm up tortillas before putting on filling to keep them from breaking.

—*Mrs. Leroy B. Miller, Middlefield, OH*

Baked Potatoes

6 or 7 fresh new potatoes
¼ c. olive oil

seasoning salt

Wash potatoes; cut into wedges (6 pieces); drain. Toss with olive oil and spread out on cookie sheet. Sprinkle with seasoning salt. Bake at 375° for 45-50 minutes or until done.

—*Norma Troyer, Middlebury, IN*

*A cheerful friend is like a sunny day, which
sends its brightness all around.*

Parslied Potatoes

1½ lbs. small new red
    potatoes, scrubbed
1 Tbsp. olive oil
1 medium onion, chopped

1 small clove garlic, chopped
1 c. chicken broth
1 c. fresh parsley, chopped
½ tsp. pepper

Heat a large skillet over medium-high heat; add oil. Sauté onion and garlic for 5 minutes or until tender. Add broth, ¾ c. parsley, and pepper; mix well. Bring to a boil. Place potatoes in a single layer in skillet. Return to a boil; reduce heat. Simmer, covered, for 10 minutes or until potatoes are tender.

—Marie Raber, Baltic, OH

Potato Cheese Pie

Crust:
2-2½ c. mashed potatoes
2 Tbsp. flour
1 tsp. baking powder
1 egg
2 Tbsp. butter, melted
salt and pepper to taste

Filling:
2 eggs
1 c. milk or cream
salt and pepper
¾ c. cheese, grated
meat, optional

Crust: Mix ingredients and pat into large greased pie pan as if dough.

Filling: Beat eggs. Add milk and seasonings. Pour into potato crust and top with cheese. Bake at 350° for 30 minutes or till knife inserted in center comes out clean. This fills a large pie pan. You may want to place the pie pan on a sheet cake pan to bake it. This works well for breakfast too!

—Mrs. Mervin H. Yoder, Pleasant Hill, IL

Potato Kugel

3-4 potatoes, peeled
2 medium carrots, peeled
1 onion
2 eggs, beaten

¾ c. milk
2 tsp. salt
⅛ tsp. sage
3 Tbsp. olive oil

Grate vegetables and drain off liquid. Stir in remaining ingredients. Spread in a glass casserole dish. Bake at 350° for 50-55 minutes.

—*Malinda Yoder, Marion, KY*

Potatoes and Spinach

1½ c. potatoes, cubed
1 c. cooked spinach
1½-2 c. milk

1 Tbsp. butter
salt and pepper to taste

Cook potatoes until soft; drain and add spinach, milk, butter, and seasonings. Serve with toast and crackers.

—*Thelma Zook, Oakland, MD*

Baked Potato Stack

Scrub potatoes or soak in fruit and vegetable rinse, then wash. Turn oven to 400°. Lay potatoes (unwrapped) on rack and bake for 1 hour. Put on plates and serve with diced green peppers, onions, sour cream, shredded cheese, meat, or topping of your choice. You may want to make a white sauce type of gravy to put on top.

—*Miriam Yoder, Baltic, OH*

Potatoes Roasted with Garlic and Onion

4 medium potatoes
2 Tbsp. olive oil
2 garlic cloves, minced

½ c. onion, thickly sliced
salt to taste
parsley

Heat oven to 400°. Scrub potatoes and cut into wedges. Toss with olive oil, garlic cloves, onion, and salt. Bake in a shallow dish until dark golden brown and fork-tender-test after 20 minutes. Sprinkle with parsley and serve.

—*Charlene Kennell, South Wayne, WI*

Golden Potato Wedges

6 large potatoes
¼ c. whole wheat flour
¼ c. Parmesan cheese, grated
¾ tsp. salt
⅛ tsp. cayenne pepper

chopped parsley, fresh or
dried
dash of garlic powder
¼ c. butter, melted on
baking sheet

Scrub or peel potatoes; cut into wedges lengthwise. Mix next 6 ingredients. In a plastic bag, add potatoes and shake well to coat. Spread in a single layer on baking sheet with melted butter. Bake at 350°-400° for 45-60 minutes or until potatoes are golden and tender with a slightly crisp coating. Turn once or twice while baking.

—*Amanda Bricker, Cass City, MI*

Right is right if nobody does it, and
wrong is wrong even if everybody does it.

Baked Potato Supper

4 baked potatoes
2 c. cooked broccoli

2 c. cooked ham, diced

White Sauce:
2 Tbsp. butter
⅓ c. flour
1½ c. milk

½ tsp. salt
½ c. cheese

Cook the ham. Dice the baked potatoes. Cook broccoli towards end of potato baking time. Serve the potatoes and pass the broccoli and ham and put sauce on top.

—*Carol Hostetler, Doylesburg, PA*

Five-Layer Dinner

2 c. raw potatoes, sliced
1 lb. hamburger
1 c. green pepper, minced
2 c. cooked tomatoes

green pepper slices
1 c. raw onion, sliced
salt and pepper

Layer potatoes, beef, onions, peppers, and tomatoes in a 2-qt. casserole dish. Season each layer with salt and pepper. Garnish with sliced green peppers. Cover and bake for 2 hours at 350°.

—*Mrs. Naomi Ruth Bontrager, Mio, MI*

Hobo Sandwiches

Fry a strip of bacon; place a piece of bread with a yolk-sized hole in the center into a pan. Break an egg into it. Fry.
Note: Tastes even better when eaten outdoors.

—*Jean Pichiya, Liberty, PA*

Hobo Helpers

In a roaster, put a thick layer of fresh cabbage, shredded. Add a layer of thickly sliced potatoes. Top with onions and carrots. Season with salt and pepper. Add more layers until full. Use cabbage only in the bottom. You can add other vegetables. Over the top put a layer of raw meat, preferably hamburger. Cover tightly with lid or foil. Bake at 375° for 1½-2 hours. Top with cheese slices before serving, optional.

—*Miriam Yoder, Baltic, OH*

Hobo Dinner

Stainless steel skillet is preferred. Fry hamburger patties on one side and turn. Add a slice of onion on each patty. Cover all with a good layer of raw shredded potatoes. Sprinkle with salt and add a little water. Cover and simmer slowly for 20 minutes or so. Once potatoes are soft, uncover and cover with cheese if desired.

—*Gertie Troyer, Loganville, WI*

Hoboes

Take a square of tinfoil and arrange cabbage leaves, fresh hamburger patty, sliced potatoes, onions, carrots, beans, or peas on top. (Use whatever vegetables you have on hand.) Add a dab of butter and salt and pepper. Wrap tinfoil securely around everything. Place on baking sheet and bake at 350° till vegetables are done. Cheese also makes it good.

—*Miss Betty Hilty, Oakfield, ME*

Bean Bake for Lumberjacks

1 lb. bacon	32 oz. kidney beans, cooked
1 c. onions, diced	16 oz. pinto beans, cooked
⅔ c. maple syrup	16 oz. Northern beans, cooked
½ tsp. dry mustard	½ tsp. pepper
1 Tbsp. garlic, minced	½ c. barbecue sauce
1 Tbsp. salt	

Fry bacon and onion. Stir in remaining ingredients. Bake until bubbly in a 350° oven, stirring a few times.

—*Mary Detweiler, West Farmington, OH*

Baked Beans

1 lb. ground beef	¾ tsp. stevia
1 large onion, chopped	2 Tbsp. mustard
5 c. beans, cooked	1 tsp. honey
2 tsp. vinegar	1 Tbsp. molasses
1½ c. ketchup	

Brown ground beef and onion together. Add the rest of ingredients. Pour into a casserole dish and bake at 400° for 30-35 minutes.

—*Mrs. John Houston, Cottage Grove, TN*

The light of the eyes rejoiceth the heart: and
a good report makes the bones fat.
—*Proverbs 15:30*

Baked Beans

2 c. beans
⅓ c. molasses
1 tsp. honey
1 Tbsp. salt

1 medium onion, chopped
dash of garlic salt
¼ c. olive oil

Soak 2 c. beans overnight; drain; cover with 1" fresh water. Cook until almost tender, then add the other ingredients. Bake in a covered dish for 3-4 hours at 350°. Uncover for last hour.

—*Mrs. Naomi Ruth Bontrager, Mio, MI*

Refried Beans

2 c. uncooked pinto beans, washed
6 c. water
2 bay leaves
1 Tbsp. ground cumin
1 tsp. ground coriander
½ tsp. cayenne
½ tsp. black pepper
½ tsp. oregano

½ tsp. basil
¼ c. butter
½ tsp. dried dill weed
2½ tsp. salt
3 Tbsp. olive oil
1 onion, chopped
1 green pepper, chopped
4 cloves garlic, chopped

Put beans, water, and bay leaves in a pot. Bring to a boil, then reduce heat and simmer, partially covered, for 2-3 hours. Stir occasionally. In a frying pan, heat oil. Add onion, green pepper, and garlic, and sauté for 3 minutes. Reduce heat; add spices and sauté for 2 minutes. Remove bay leaves and mash beans. Mash in the vegetable-spice mixture, then add butter. Continue to cook over very low heat for 30 minutes to blend flavors. Stir often. Yield: 6 c.

—*Bertha Peachey, Hamptonville, NC*

Flavorful Dressing

1 loaf whole wheat bread,
   cubed and toasted
6 eggs, beaten
3 c. milk
1 small onion, finely chopped
2 tsp. salt

2 tsp. chicken base
1 pt. cooked chicken, chopped
1 pt. mixed vegetables,
   cooked and cubed
1 tsp. garlic salt
1 stick butter

Melt butter in bottom of medium-sized roaster. Combine all ingredients and pour into roaster. Bake at 350° for 1 hour or until almost dry, or fry in pan on stove top.

—*Mrs. Vernon Hershberger, Loganville, WI*

Bulgur Stuffing

¼ c. olive oil
4 c. bulgur wheat
2 qt. stock, hot
1 onion, chopped
4 stalks celery, chopped
2 tsp. salt

¼ c. nutritional yeast
6 Tbsp. parsley flakes
½ tsp. tarragon
½ tsp. thyme
½ tsp. basil

Heat oil. Sauté bulgur; gradually add stock. Cover and simmer 10 minutes with onion. Add remaining ingredients. Simmer 5 minutes more. Let cool. This will stuff 2 4-5 lb. fowl. Also good for stuffed vegetables. You may want to serve this as a main dish casserole in place of rice.

—*Cyndi Davis, Flemingsburg, KY*

The Lord is pleased with your little, if it is the best you have.

Polenta

4½ c. milk
1½ c. yellow cornmeal
2 Tbsp. butter
⅓ c. onion, finely chopped
¼ c. carrot, finely chopped
2 cloves garlic, minced
1 Tbsp. fresh parsley, chopped
1½ tsp. chopped fresh basil
   or ¼ tsp. dried basil
¾ tsp. fresh oregano or ¼ tsp. dried oregano

1 bay leaf
3 c. canned tomatoes,
   partially drained
½ tsp. salt
¼ tsp. pepper
8 oz. provolone cheese,
thinly sliced
1½ c. dry cottage cheese,
mixed with 1 c. sour cream

Bring milk to a boil in a heavy saucepan. Reduce to simmer; add cornmeal in a thin, steady stream, stirring constantly. Stir over medium heat about 10 minutes until mixture is thick. Cover; simmer very slowly 40 more minutes, stirring occasionally and adding ¼ cup water (when using homemade cornmeal, more water may be needed) several times as necessary. Pour into lightly buttered pan 9" x 5". Let cool. Melt butter in 3-qt. saucepan. Add onion, carrot, garlic, parsley, basil, oregano, and bay leaf. Sauté about 5 minutes; stir in tomatoes, salt, and pepper. Simmer until thickened, about 20 minutes. Discard bay leaf. Preheat oven to 400°. Invert cooked polenta on cutting board and cut in ½" thick slices. Spread a cup of sauce in bottom of a 13" casserole dish. Arrange polenta and cheese in overlapping layers. Spoon with remaining sauce and top with curd cheese. Bake 25-30 minutes or until lightly browned.

—*Lydia Lapp, Cassadaga, NY*

Greatness does not consist in never falling,
but in rising every time you fall.

Borscht

1 c. beets	2 c. beef or chicken stock
1 c. carrots	1 c. cabbage
1 c. onions	1 Tbsp. lemon juice
1 Tbsp. butter	1 Tbsp. thick sour cream, optional

Peel beets and cut finely. Cut carrots and onions finely. Barely cover with boiling water. Simmer, covered, for 15 minutes. Add butter, stock, and finely cut cabbage and boil 15 more minutes. Stir in lemon juice. Put in bowls. Add 1 Tbsp. thick sour cream to each bowl if desired.

Variation: ½-1 cup of tomato pulp may be used instead of lemon juice.

—*Lydia Lapp, Cassadaga, NY*

Haystack Meal

1 bag corn chips, slightly crumbled	1 qt. cheese sauce
1 large onion, chopped	1 head lettuce, chopped
2 lb. hamburger	2 c. tomatoes, diced
taco seasoning	1 c. peppers, diced
2 qt. cooked brown rice	1 c. onions, diced
2-3 c. cooked pinto beans	cheese, shredded, optional

Fry onion with hamburger and season with taco seasoning. Each person builds their own haystack (stacking one item on top of the other) on their plate in order given and top with your favorite salad dressing and cheese sauce. Some dollops of plain yogurt or sour cream is also good.

—*Mrs. Elmer Esh, Burkesville, KY*

Hot Cabbage Slaw

9 c. cabbage, finely shredded
1 egg
1 tsp. salt
pepper to taste
2 Tbsp. honey
¼ c. vinegar

Shred cabbage finely and add boiling water to cover. Cook 5 minutes. Drain. Beat egg and add honey, vinegar, salt, and pepper. Add to drained cabbage. Heat thoroughly 5 minutes. Add ½ tsp. caraway seeds if you like.

—Mrs. Leroy Auker, Elk Horn, KY

Baked Cabbage

1 small head cabbage, shredded

White Sauce:
3 Tbsp. butter or olive oil
2 Tbsp. (rounded) whole
    wheat flour
1½-2 c. milk
salt and pepper
Parmesan cheese
bread crumbs

Cook cabbage in salt water until tender. Drain and put cabbage in a Pyrex casserole. To make white sauce: Melt butter in pan; add flour and brown lightly. Add milk a little at a time. Cook until thick and bubbly. Season with salt and pepper. Pour over cabbage; sprinkle with Parmesan and bread crumbs. Cover and bake at 350° for 15-20 minutes or until bubbly around edges.

—Mrs. Leroy B. Miller, Middlefield, OH

Never answer an angry word with an angry word,
it's the second one that makes the quarrel.

Skillet Dinner

¼ c. butter	3 c. cooked brown rice
½ c. onion, chopped	½ c. sunflower seeds
1 c. celery, chopped	½ c. almonds, sliced
½ large green pepper, chopped	2 tsp. coriander
10 mushrooms, sliced	salt and pepper to taste

Topping:
2 ripe tomatoes, chunked   ½ lb. (or less) cheese, grated

Using a stainless steel skillet with a tight-fitting lid, sauté vegetables and mushrooms in butter. Add the rest of ingredients and blend. Top with tomatoes and cheese. Cover and heat long enough to melt cheese.

—*Mrs. Junior Detweiler, Redding, IA*

Sunday Dinner Rice Dish

1 lb. hamburger	1½ c. water
2 onions, chopped	1½ c. uncooked brown rice
1 c. celery, chopped	1 tsp. salt
8 oz. cream of chicken soup	½ tsp. pepper
8 oz. cream of mushroom soup	

Brown hamburger, onions, and celery. Add the rest of ingredients. Put in Crock-Pot before leaving for church. Come home to dinner already made.

—*Mrs. John Houston, Cottage Grove, TN*

It is much better to hold out a hand than to point a finger.

Rice Medley

2 qt. cooked brown rice	**½ c. carrots, shredded**
½ c. onion, chopped	**½-1 c. cooked chicken or**
½ c. celery, chopped	**turkey, diced**

Simmer in broth or water until vegetables are tender. Season to taste with chicken soup base or garlic salt or powder.

—Mrs. Mervin H. Yoder, Pleasant Hill, IL

Rice Colorful

Cook 1 c. brown rice in 2 c. water and 1 tsp. sea salt. Heat ¼ c. oil in a skillet. Add the cooked rice, ½ c. chopped green onions, and ½ c. diced green pepper. Sauté until vegetables are tender-crisp. Fork-toss with 3 Tbsp. diced pimento and ½ c. sliced ripe olives. For added flavor serve with vegetable seasoning.

—Laura Yoder, Free Union, VA

Chicken, Veggies, and Rice

Cut up 2 c. chicken breasts in cubes and fry in pan 7-10 minutes. Add 4 c. water and simmer a little, then add vegetables of your choice such as onions, green beans, carrots, cabbage, peppers, shredded zucchini, or peas. Add salt and pepper to taste. Cook till vegetables are soft, then serve over cooked brown rice. You may need to thicken it a little with flour or cornstarch mixed with a little water.

—Mrs. Leroy Esh, Burkesville, KY

Chicken and Rice

1 c. brown rice	garlic as you like
1⅓ c. water	½ c. celery, chopped
1⅓ c. milk	½ c. onions, chopped
2 tsp. salt	1 raw chicken, cut up
½ tsp. pepper	paprika to taste

Stir all ingredients except chicken in medium-sized roaster pan. Lay pieces of chicken on top. Season chicken with salt, pepper, and paprika. Cover and bake at 350° for 2-2½ hours depending on the size of the chicken pieces. Take out and serve chicken on platter and rice in bowl. Rice will be tasty and moist.

—Mary E. Beachy, Liberty, KY

Italian Chicken Medley

2 Tbsp. olive oil	2 tsp. vinegar
1½ lb. fresh or frozen white	1 tsp. garlic powder
chicken meat, cut in strips	1 tsp. dried sweet basil
1½ c. celery, sliced ¼"	1 tsp. dried oregano
1½ c. green pepper, chopped	½ tsp. black pepper
½ c. onion, chopped	1½ c. long-cooking rice of
2 qt. whole tomatoes	your choice
2 tsp. parsley leaves	salt to taste

In a heavy 6-qt. stainless steel pan, sauté the chicken strips in olive oil over medium heat till juices run clear. Remove from pan; add celery, pepper, and onion; cook until tender. Return chicken to pan and add remaining ingredients. Cover and simmer 30 minutes. Check – more liquid may be needed for rice. I add tomato juice. If you use brown rice, increase simmering time.

—Cathy Hochstetler, Nappanee, IN

Easy Taco Skillet Meal

1 lb. ground beef	¾ c. water
1 pt. tomato juice	2 Tbsp. maple syrup
1 c. uncooked rice	1 pkg. taco seasoning
1 c. cheddar cheese, shredded	

Brown beef in a large skillet with lid. Add tomato juice, water, seasonings, and rice. Simmer 45 minutes or until rice is tender, stirring several times. Top with shredded cheese. Serve with shredded lettuce, onions, sour cream, and salsa.

—Mrs. Johnny Miller, Loudonville, OH

Crispy Onions

1 Tbsp. honey	3 Tbsp. lemon juice

Slice an onion with V slicer; spread out on dinner plate. Sprinkle onions with Real salt. Mix honey and lemon juice; pour over onions. Let set 15 minutes. Sprinkle with oregano. The children prefer this over pizza. They will not eat only onion, but this will turn a strong onion into a sweet crispy ring. Some people use vinegar, but I like the lemon juice.

—Mrs. Samuel Stoltzfus, Howard, PA

Green Beans

Sauté ⅓ c. chopped onions in 2 Tbsp. butter. Drain 1 qt. green beans and add to the onions. Season with ½ tsp. Real salt. Stir and heat through.

—Mrs. Raymond Yutzy, Howe, IN

Toasty Green Beans

Heat a skillet with 2 Tbsp. butter. Add 2 slices bread, finely cubed. Brown. Add 1 qt. canned green beans, drained. Add salt and pepper. Cook until heated through. You may want to add some bean water so it's not too dry.

—Mrs. Junior Detweiler, Redding, IA

Baked Carrots

1 qt. carrots, shredded   3 Tbsp. water
2 Tbsp. onion, finely minced   salt and pepper to taste

Combine carrots, onion, and water in an oven-safe dish or casserole dish. Sprinkle lightly with salt and pepper if desired. Cover and bake at 375° for ½ hour for moist, delicious carrots.

—Amanda Bricker, Cass City, MI

Carrots

5-6 medium-sized carrots   3 Tbsp. maple syrup
3 Tbsp. butter   ½ tsp. ginger

Slice carrots and cook until tender. Combine butter and maple syrup. Heat until not quite boiling. Stir in ginger. Pour over carrots.

—Miriam Hershberger, Middlefield, OH

*"Friendship" consists of forgetting what one gives
and remembering what one receives.*

Garlicky Steamed Veggies

2 Tbsp. olive oil (preferably extra virgin)
1 onion, sliced
2 small garlic cloves, minced
1 c. baby carrots or carrot chunks

3 Tbsp. water
1 small zucchini, chunked
1 c. broccoli flowerets

In a medium saucepan heat olive oil. Add onion and garlic. Fry a minute or two on medium heat. Add carrots and water. Cover and steam until just beginning to soften. Add zucchini and broccoli. Do not stir. Cover and steam several minutes longer until vegetables are crisp tender. Salt to taste. Stir. Serve.

—*Charlene Kennell, South Wayne, WI*

Banana Peppers with Onions

Dice 1 medium onion and put in Corningware or Pyrex pan. Add enough olive oil to coat onions. Fry lightly, with lid on, till onions are limp. Add cut-up banana peppers, enough to fill your pan. Stir and heat slowly with lid on. Having your pan full will help to not burn them. Heat till peppers have changed colors. Salt may be added. Serve hot. Leftovers are good to add to fresh cut-up tomatoes plus balsamic vinegar and basil herb or whatever else you'd like to add for a salad.

—*Ella Stutzman, Wyoming, DE*

And make me savoury meat, such as I love, and bring it to me,
that I may eat; that my soul may bless thee before I die.
—*Genesis 27:4*

Garden Vegetable Tomato Sauce

3 Tbsp. olive oil
3 garlic cloves, minced
1 c. onion, chopped
½ c. carrot, chopped
1 c. fennel bulb, chopped
½ c. celery, chopped
1 c. pepper, chopped

1½ c. mushrooms, sliced
2 tsp. salt
⅛ tsp. black pepper
4 c. tomato puree
2 c. squash, chopped
½ c. fresh basil, minced

Sauté olive oil and garlic for 1 minute on medium heat. Increase heat to high and add onion, carrot, fennel, celery, pepper, mushrooms, salt, and pepper, and sauté 8-10 minutes. Mix in tomato puree and reduce heat to low. Simmer 40 minutes. Add squash and cook 5 minutes. Add basil. Serve over pasta. This recipe doesn't need to be followed exactly. Any vegetable makes it good!

—Bertha Peachey, Hamptonville, NC

Pennsylvania Dutch Corn Pie

pastry for pie (top and
   bottom crust)
2 c. fresh corn
2 Tbsp. whole wheat flour
1 Tbsp. parsley, chopped

2 hard-boiled eggs
1 Tbsp. butter
½ c. milk
salt and pepper

Sprinkle flour on bottom shell of pie. Add corn and remaining ingredients. Cover with remaining crust and crimp edge. Cut vents in top crust. Bake 45 minutes at 375°.

—Mrs. Leroy Auker, Elk Horn, KY

Corn Pie

4 c. fresh corn
⅛ tsp. celery salt
1 Tbsp. butter
½-¾ c. milk

2 eggs, beaten
1-2 c. smoked sausage
1 Tbsp. flour, optional
1 pie crust (top and bottom)

Mix all together except meat. Put into pie crust. Add smoked sausage. Put on top crust. Bake at 350° until top is golden.

—*Mary Nolt, Withee, WI*

Dried Corn

8 pt. corn
½ c. maple syrup

1 c. milk or cream
3 Tbsp. salt

Mix together in heavy saucepan and cook 20 minutes, then put on drying pan. Keep well stirred and be careful not to burn it when it's almost dry.

—*Jolene Bontrager, Hillsboro, WI*

Baked Dried Corn

1 c. dried corn
2 c. hot milk
2 eggs, beaten
1 c. milk

1 tsp. butter
1 Tbsp. honey
salt and pepper

Mix corn and 2 c. milk. Let stand 1 hour. Add eggs, milk, butter, and honey. Season with salt and pepper to taste. Bake ½ hour or longer in 350° oven.

—*Mrs. Reuben Troyer, Rich Hill, MO*

Creamed Hominy

1 qt. hominy

1 pt. fried sausage

½ tsp. pepper

milk or cream

2 Tbsp. whole wheat flour

Cover hominy, sausage, and pepper with milk or cream. Bring to a boil. Thicken with flour.

—Lydia Hostetler, Danville, OH

Hominy

Wash 1 gal. shelled field corn, cover with cold water, and add 5 heaping Tbsp. soda. Mix well. Soak overnight in a cool place. In morning, put on stove and add more water so corn is covered. Cook until hulls or skins come off. Add water as needed. When corn is soft, wash off hulls, changing water often. Cover with water and let soak overnight again or until it doesn't taste like soda. To can, fill jars only a little over half full as it'll really swell up yet. Add 1 tsp. salt per quart. Pressure cook 30 minutes at 10 lbs. pressure.

—Lydia Hostetler, Danville, OH

Perhaps the best way to live happily ever after is not to be after too much.

Casseroles

Cabbage Casserole

1 medium head cabbage
1½ c. cooked brown rice
1 pt. tomato soup

1 lb. ground beef or turkey
1 lb. cheese, grated

Brown ground beef; drain grease. Add tomato soup and rice. Set aside. Cut cabbage as for slaw. Pre-boil just until tender; drain off water. Mix with ground beef mixture. Layer in casserole dish with cheese, finishing with cheese. Bake at 350° for 1 hour or until done.

—*Mary E. Showalter, Mt. Solon, VA*

Chicken Sauerkraut Casserole

4 large potatoes, peeled and grated
2-3 c. cooked chicken, diced

2 Tbsp. onion, diced finely
1 qt. homemade sauerkraut

Grease an 8" x 10" casserole dish with olive oil. Peel, grate, and rinse potatoes and layer in casserole dish. Add the onion; layer chicken meat next. Put sauerkraut on top and bake at 350° for 1 hour.

—*Carol Hostetler, Doylesburg, PA*

Chicken Rice Broccoli Casserole

1 qt. chicken broth
½ qt. chicken pieces
1 pt. broccoli, frozen or fresh
2 tsp. parsley

⅔ c. rice
2 c. water
¾ c. cheese, optional
2 Tbsp. onion, chopped

Put all in casserole dish or roaster and bake at 275° for 3 hours. This is very nice for a company meal.

—*Carol Hostetler, Doylesburg, PA*

Shipwreck

1 qt. potatoes, diced	¼ c. uncooked rice
1 c. celery, diced	1 lb. hamburger
1 onion, chopped	1 tsp. salt
1 can tomatoes	1 tsp. pepper
1 can kidney beans	1½ c. (or more) water

Mix and put all ingredients in casserole dish. Put on lid or cover with foil and bake at 350° for 1½ hours. Remove cover and bake another ½ hour.

—Gertie Troyer, Loganville, WI

Herbed Harvest Veggie Casserole

4 new potatoes, cut in ¼" slices	½ c. uncooked long
1 Tbsp. fresh sage, chopped,	grain rice
or 1 tsp. dried	3 medium zucchini, thinly
1 Tbsp. fresh tarragon,	sliced
chopped, or 1 tsp. dried	1 c. tomatoes, thinly sliced
¼ c. butter	Swiss or other cheese of
3 medium sweet bell	choice
peppers, seeded and diced	salt, pepper, and garlic
1 onion, thinly sliced	salt to taste

Grease 2½-qt. casserole dish (with lid). Arrange half of potatoes in overlapping rows. Dot with half of the butter; sprinkle with half of the spices, and half each of the onion, peppers, and zucchini. Sprinkle all of rice on top. Then repeat layers of butter, potatoes, spices, peppers, onion, and zucchini. Cover and bake at 350° for 1½ hours or until potatoes are tender. Remove from oven; top with tomato slices, then cheese. Bake uncovered 10 minutes more till cheese is melted. Let stand 10 minutes. Yields: 6-8 servings.

—Brenda Gause, Tippecanoe, IN

Casserole of Vegetables

4 c. stock (chicken or beef)	1 c. tomatoes
or 5 c. tomato juice	1 c. peas
1 c. uncooked brown rice	1 tsp. parsley
4 c. potatoes, sliced thin	1 tsp. basil
1 onion, thinly sliced	1 tsp. oregano

Put all ingredients into a casserole. Cover and bake in a slow oven (300°) until rice is tender.

—*Mrs. Leroy Auker, Elk Horn, KY*

Vegetable Casserole

½ lb. whole wheat noodles	1 c. canned sweet corn
1 medium onion, chopped	1 qt. whole tomatoes
1 green pepper, chopped	1 tsp. sea salt
1 c. mushrooms, sliced	¾ lb. raw cheddar cheese,
½ c. sliced green olives	grated

Bring 1 qt. water to a boil in a large stainless steel saucepan. Add noodles and cook until they are tender. Drain noodles and place in a casserole dish. Add other ingredients and top with grated cheese. Bake in a 350° oven for 30-45 minutes.

—*Mary S. Yoder, Wooster, OH*

A heart at peace gives life to the body.
—*Proverbs 14:30*

There is a sermon in a smile.

Burrito Casserole

2 lb. hamburger	2 c. sour cream
2 pkg. taco seasoning	10 soft tortilla shells
1 pt. refried beans	1 pkg. cheddar cheese
3 c. cream of mushroom soup	

Brown hamburger with onions. Add taco mix and beans; simmer 5 minutes. Mix mushroom soup and sour cream together. Put half of soup mixture in a 2" x 9" x 13" pan. Tear the tortilla shells up and layer on soup mixture. Put meat mixture on top of tortilla shells. Spread remaining soup mixture on top and sprinkle with a little cheese. Bake for 1 hour at 325°. Add rest of cheese and melt. Serve with lettuce, tomatoes, and onions, or salsa.

—*Mrs. Raymond Yutzy, Howe, IN*

Garden Casserole

2 qt. ½" whole wheat bread cubes	1 lb. ground beef
2 c. cheese, grated	salt and pepper to taste
⅓ c. butter, melted	1 medium onion, chopped
1 pt. peas or beans, cooked and drained	¼ c. whole wheat flour
	2 c. milk

Toss together bread cubes, cheese, and butter until blended. Press 3 cups of this mixture into a 9" x 13" pan. Flatten and press thin to cover the bottom of the pan. Spread vegetables over bread layer. Brown meat and onion. Drain. Stir in flour and mix well. Remove from heat; add seasonings and milk. Stir until smooth. Return to low heat and cook until thickened. Layer over veggies. Top with rest of bread/cheese mixture. Bake at 350° for 25 minutes or until browned. May be frozen but must be thoroughly thawed before baking.

—*Iva Kauffman, Monroe, WI*

Zucchini Casserole

1 qt. hamburger	9 slices bread, cubed
½ c. onion, chopped	3 Tbsp. butter
1 pt. pizza sauce	½ tsp. Italian seasoning or
1 medium zucchini, shoestring	herbs of your choice
½ tsp. salt	cheese
½ tsp. oregano	

Brown the hamburger and onion in a skillet. Add pizza sauce and oregano. Pour into a 9" x 13" glass pan. Top with shredded zucchini and sprinkle with salt. Cover and bake at 350° for ½ hour. In the meantime, melt butter in a heavy skillet. Add cubed bread and seasonings. Stir to coat evenly and until lightly toasted. Arrange on top of zucchini; cover with cheese; return to oven and bake uncovered for 10 more minutes. Serve immediately.

—Mrs. Raymond Yutzy, Howe, IN

Zucchini-Egg Casserole

4 c. zucchini, shredded finely	1 pt. hamburger, crumbled
1 medium onion, chopped	1 tsp. salt
4 eggs	cheese
1 c. cream	

Beat the eggs and cream until well blended. Pour over zucchini, onion, meat, and salt. Stir well to mix. Pour into 9" x 13" glass cake pan. Bake uncovered at 350° for 40 minutes. Cover with shredded cheese and return to oven till cheese is melted.

—Mrs. Raymond Yutzy, Howe, IN

Kindness is shown by the words we speak,
and in the tone in which we speak them.

Hamburger Brown Rice Casserole

2 c. brown rice
5 c. water
16 hamburger patties

1 c. celery, diced, or 1 pt. cream of celery soup
salt to taste

Bring rice, water, salt, and raw celery or soup to a boil. Meanwhile, fry hamburger. Place rice in roaster. Top with hamburgers. Cover roaster. Bake 1 hour at 350°.

—Mrs. Allen A. Bontrager, LaGrange, IN

California Casserole

2 lb. beef chunks (may use canned)
⅓ c. whole wheat flour
1 tsp. paprika
¼ c. butter
½ tsp. salt
⅛ tsp. pepper
1 c. meat broth
1 can cream of chicken soup
1¾ c. water
1¾ c. onion, diced

Dumplings:
1¾ c. whole wheat flour
¼ c. wheat germ
4 tsp. baking powder
½ tsp. salt
1 tsp. poultry seasoning
1 tsp. celery seed
1 tsp. onion flakes
¼ c. oil
1-1¼ c. milk

Coat beef chunks with flour and paprika. Brown in butter and add salt and pepper. Add meat broth and pour into a 3-qt. baking dish. Heat soup, water, and onions and add to meat in casserole. Drop dumplings on top and bake at 425° until dumplings are done (15-20 minutes).
Dumplings: Mix all ingredients in order given just until blended.
—Mrs. Leroy B. Miller, Middlefield, OH

Chicken Gumbo

2½ qt. cooked potatoes, cubed
2-3 carrots, diced and cooked
1 soup
2 loaves bread, toasted and
   cubed
1 dozen eggs
1 onion, chopped

3 sticks celery, chopped
24 oz. cream of chicken
   soup
salt, pepper, and poultry
   seasoning to taste
½ c. butter, browned
milk to make it moist

Mix all together. Pour into a baking dish and bake at 300° for 3 hours.

I don't always cook the vegetables. Just mix them in and bake at 300° for 4 hours. Can add some peas also. Sometimes I use broth to make it moist instead of milk.

—*Mrs. John Houston, Cottage Grove, TN*

Classic Ratatouille

¼ c. olive oil or butter
2 medium onions, chopped
2 cloves garlic, minced
2 small eggplants, cut into
   1" cubes
3 small zucchini, sliced
3 stalks celery, thinly sliced
1 sweet red pepper, cored, seeded, and cut into ½" cubes
1 sweet green pepper, cored, seeded, and cut into ½" cubes

4 plum tomatoes, quartered
1 Tbsp. fresh basil,
   chopped, or ½ tsp. dried
2 Tbsp. packed fresh
   parsley, minced
1 tsp. dried oregano
½ tsp. dried thyme, optional

In a heavy skillet, heat 2 Tbsp. oil or butter; add onions and garlic. Cook until soft, but not browned. Add eggplants, zucchini, red pepper, green pepper, celery, tomatoes, and remaining oil or butter. Cover and cook gently over low heat 30 minutes. Add spices. Cover and cook 10 minutes or until most of the liquid has evaporated and mixture is thick. 1 qt. canned meat can be added if preferred. This is good eaten with rice, spaghetti, or noodles.

—*Jolene Bontrager, Hillsboro, WI*

Squash and Apple Bake

squash or neck pumpkin,   ¼ c. butter, melted
    peel and cut into 1" rings   1 Tbsp. flour
2-3 (more if desired) apples,   ½ tsp. salt
    peel, core, and rice   ½ tsp. cinnamon
½ c. maple syrup or ⅓ c. honey

Arrange squash in 9" x 13" baking pan. Combine apples with remaining ingredients and spoon over squash. Bake at 350° for 1 hour.

Variations: Squash can be substituted with sweet potatoes for a tasty dish.

—*Jolene Bontrager, Hillsboro, WI*

Mexican Corn Casserole

4 eggs, beaten   ¼ c. olive oil
1 qt. canned corn, drained   1 onion, chopped
1½ c. cornmeal   green chilies, diced, optional
1¼ c. buttermilk   1 tsp. baking soda
½ c. butter, melted   3 c. cheese, shredded

Mix all ingredients. Pour into a 9" x 13" dish. Bake 1 hour at 325°. Let stand 15 minutes before serving. Serve with salsa.

—*Mary Showalter, Mt. Solon, VA*

And honey, and butter, and sheep, and cheese of kine, for David, and for the people that were with him, to eat...
—*II Samuel 17:29*

Good-for-You Chili

4 c. water
28 oz. canned tomatoes,
   crushed
32 oz. pinto or red kidney
   beans, rinsed and drained
16 oz. solid pack pumpkin
1 c. onion, chopped
⅔ c. bulgur wheat, uncooked

4 oz. chopped green
   chilies, optional
2½ Tbsp. chili powder
1 c. red bell pepper,
   chopped, optional
1 tsp. cumin
1 tsp. salt
1 tsp. minced garlic

Put all ingredients in a 4-5-qt. pot. Bring to a boil, reduce heat, and simmer uncovered for 30-35 minutes until bulgur is tender. Serve garnishes at table.

Garnish: sour cream or plain yogurt, shredded cheddar cheese, and sliced scallions or chopped onions.

—*Cyndi Davis, Flemingsburg, KY*

Baked Squash or Sweet Potatoes

Wash vegetables. Cut squash in half lengthwise, place cut side down on cookie sheet and bake at 350° for 1 hour. Sweet potatoes can be baked whole, but takes up to 2 hours. When soft, scoop out flesh; serve with homemade butter, salt, pepper, and nutritional yeast. Or smother with thick chili soup or vegetable soup.

—*Mrs. Junior Detweiler, Redding, IA*

Chicken Pot Pie

1 pt. chicken broth
1 pt. water
2 Tbsp. cornstarch
½ c. water
½ c. cooked potatoes, chopped

½ c. cooked carrots,
   chopped
¼ c. cooked onion, chopped
salt and pepper

Pour into a 9" x 13" pan. Top with Melt-in-Your-Mouth Biscuits. Bake at 400° until golden. Serve with applesauce and cottage cheese.

—*Mrs. Junior Detweiler, Redding, IA*

Squash Casserole

1 lb. summer squash,	2 eggs, beaten
peeled and cubed	1 c. cheese, grated
1 small onion, sliced	1 c. whole wheat bread
3 Tbsp. butter	crumbs
1 c. milk	salt and pepper to taste

Combine first 2 ingredients; cook, drain, and mash. Add remaining ingredients, reserving ½ c. cheese to sprinkle over top. Pour into a greased pan. Bake at 350° until firm and cheese is browned. You may want to cook vegetables in very little water, then use that water for part of the milk.

—*Mary E. Showalter, Mt. Solon, VA*

Dinner in a Dish

2 lb. hamburger	1 qt. tomato chunks
2 large onions, chopped	1 Tbsp. salt
1 qt. corn	¼ c. honey

Brown hamburger with onions. Add rest of ingredients and cook for a few minutes. May be served as a stew. A cup of whole wheat bread crumbs may be added to soak up most of the juice, then poured into a baking dish and baked at 350° for about ½ hour or until done.

Note: Grated cheese may be sprinkled on top for a nice brown topping.

—*Mary E. Showalter, Mt. Solon, VA*

I learned more about the economy from one South Dakota dust storm than I did in all my years of college.
—Hubert Humphrey

Beef Nacho Casserole

3 lb. ground beef, browned	3 Tbsp. chili powder
1 qt. (32 oz.) salsa	6 c. corn chips, crushed
1 qt. corn	6 c. Cojack, Cheddar, or
1½ c. mayonnaise	mozzarella cheese, shredded

Mix first five ingredients. Put half in bottom of a large casserole dish. Next put in half of chips, then half of cheese. Repeat layers. Bake until heated through. May top with lettuce and tomatoes.

Note: Omit chili powder if salsa is hot.

—*Mrs. Mervin H. Yoder, Pleasant Hill, IL*

Sweet Potato Casserole

4 c. sweet potatoes, cooked and mashed	3 Tbsp. butter, softened
	1 tsp. salt
3 Tbsp. maple syrup	½ c. crushed pineapple

Mix all ingredients in a mixing bowl. Then place in a 1½-qt. greased baking dish. Bake at 350° until heated through. Great dish with turkey at Thanksgiving. Can be mixed and frozen ahead of time. Just thaw and heat.

—*Mary Showalter, Mt. Solon, VA*

Easy Hamburger Quiche

1 unbaked 9" deep-dish pie crust	3 eggs
	⅓ c. homemade mayonnaise
½ lb. hamburger	½ tsp. salt
1 c. cheese, grated	⅛ tsp. black pepper
⅓ c. onion, chopped	1 Tbsp. flour
½ c. milk	

Brown hamburger and drain. Add cheese and onion and put mixture in pie crust. Mix rest of ingredients and beat until smooth. Pour over mixture in crust. Bake at 350° for 35-40 minutes or until knife inserted comes out clean.

—*Mary Showalter, Mt. Solon, VA*

Dip the spoon in hot water to measure lard, butter, etc. and the fat will slip out more easily.

Rinse a pan in cold water before scalding milk to prevent sticking.

A drink of vinegar is a sure cure for fainting.

Fresh tomatoes will keep longer if placed with stems down.

Add a small amount of vinegar to water when washing vegetables to freshen them.

Limp celery may be crisped by placing in a pan of cold water, adding a slice of potatoes, and refrigerating for several hours.

Add vinegar to water when cold packing meat to keep cans free from grease.

Put a handful of soda in scalding water to scald chickens. This will help remove pinfeathers.

A quick way to clean smudged eyeglasses is with white vinegar. A small squeeze bottle in your purse or desk allows for quick wipes with a tissue.

NOTES

_____

_____

_____

_____

_____

_____

_____

_____

_____

_____

_____

_____

_____

_____

_____

_____

_____

_____

_____

_____

_____

Pizza, Tacos, & Noodles

Pizza Crust

1 egg, beaten
⅔ c. milk
½ c. butter
2 c. whole wheat flour

½ tsp. soda
2 tsp. honey
½ tsp. salt

Mix all together lightly. Press in a 12" x 14" pan. Top with your favorite pizza toppings. Bake 25-30 minutes in a 350° oven.

—*Mrs. Junior Detweiler, Redding, IA*

Herb Pizza Crust

1 Tbsp. honey
1 Tbsp. oregano
½ Tbsp. garlic powder
1 c. warm water

1 Tbsp. salt
1 Tbsp. basil
1 Tbsp. yeast
2½ c. whole wheat flour

Mix honey, water, and yeast. Let stand 10 minutes until bubbly. Mix in seasonings, then add flour gradually until a smooth, elastic ball of dough is formed. Knead on floured board a few minutes. Use fingers or rolling pin to spread on pizza pan or cookie sheet. Bake at 350° for 15-20 minutes or till crust is done. Top with pizza sauce, cheese, and your choice of toppings.

—*Cyndi Davis, Flemingsburg, KY*

> *But godliness with contentment is great gain. For we brought nothing into this world, and it is certain we can carry nothing out. And having food and raiment let us therewith be content.*
> —*I Timothy 6:6-8*

Whole Wheat Pizza

Crust:
1 Tbsp. dry yeast
1 c. warm water
1 tsp. honey
1½ tsp. sea salt
2 Tbsp. olive oil
2½ c. whole wheat flour

Topping:
2 c. tomato sauce
1 tsp. oregano
1 c. green peppers, chopped
1 c. onions, chopped
1 c. mushrooms, sliced
½ c. sliced green olives
1 lb. mozzarella cheese,
shredded

Dissolve dry yeast in warm water. Stir in honey, sea salt, and oil. Beat in 2 c. flour. Then stir in remaining flour and knead. Put in greased bowl and cover. Let rise in warm place until double in bulk (about 1 hour). Grease pizza pans lightly. Press dough over bottom and sides of pan. Brush with oil to seal dough and keep it firm. Add topping. Mix tomato sauce and oregano together and spread over dough. Sprinkle with peppers, onions, mushrooms, and olives. Top with cheese. Bake at 425° for 15-20 minutes.

—*Mary S. Yoder, Wooster, OH*

Baked Vegetable Pizza

1½ c. whole wheat flour
½ c. roasted cornmeal
2 tsp. baking powder

¼ c. olive oil
⅔ c. water

Mix all together and press into pizza pan. Spread pizza sauce on, and top with a quart of mixed vegetables that have been cooked and ready to use. Bake at 350° for 15-20 minutes. A few minutes before it is done put some chopped peppers and grated cheese on, then finish baking.

Note: For a very tasty crust, add a little chopped onions and sweet basil flakes.

—*Irene Mae Yoder, Oakland, MD*

Toppings for Large Pizzas (12" x 14)

1½ lb. hamburger or ¾ qt.
  canned hamburger
1 tsp. salt
½ c. onions, chopped
1 small can mushrooms, chopped

1 pt. pizza sauce
1 c. cream of mushroom soup
1 lb. cheese, shredded
oregano

Fry the onion and mushrooms with the hamburger. Season with salt. Spread cream of mushroom soup evenly over pizza crust then pour on pizza sauce. Put on meat mixture and sprinkle oregano over meat. Top with shredded cheese.

—*Mrs. Raymond Yutzy, Howe, IN*

Biscuit Pizza

¼ c. butter
½ c. onions, chopped
1 qt. hamburger
¾ c. flour
1½ pt. tomato juice
1 pt. pizza sauce

1 pt. cream of mushroom soup
1 tsp. salt
1 tsp. oregano
biscuit dough (approx.
  4 c. dough)
cheese

In a 6 qt.-kettle, melt butter and fry onions. Add hamburger; chop fine and heat through. Add flour and stir well. Add tomato juice, 1 c. at a time, stirring well after each addition. Add pizza sauce and mushroom soup. If it is too thick add milk or water for right consistency. Add seasonings. Pour into roaster and drop your favorite biscuit dough on top by tablespoons. Bake at 375° for 15 minutes. Cover with cheese last 5 minutes. You can also keep your sauce in the kettle and drop the biscuits same as for roaster. Cover and let steam on low heat for 10 minutes.

—*Mrs. Raymond Yutzy, Howe, IN*

Corn Bread Pizza

1 c. cornmeal	½ c. onion, chopped
1 c. flour	1 pt. pork and beans
4 tsp. baking powder	1 small can mushrooms
½ tsp. salt	1 pt. pizza sauce
1 egg	1 pt. cream of mushroom soup
¼ c. oil	½ tsp. oregano
1 c. milk	salt and pepper to taste
1½ lb. hamburger	cheese

Mix together cornmeal, flour, baking powder, and salt. Add egg, oil, and milk and beat well. Spread in a greased 9" x 13" cake pan and bake at 375° for 15-20 minutes. In the meantime, fry the hamburger with the onion (if canned meat is used, use ¾ qt.); add beans, mushrooms, pizza sauce, and mushroom soup. Add seasonings. Pour over corn bread, cover with cheese, and bake until cheese is well melted or about 10 minutes.

—*Mrs. Raymond Yutzy, Howe, IN*

Tacos

¾ c. cornmeal	1½ c. water
1 c. whole wheat flour	2 eggs
1 tsp. salt	1½ Tbsp. oil

Mix well. Roll out paper thin using ¼ c. at a time. Fry in an ungreased skillet on both sides.

—*Elva Troyer, Scottsville, KY*

Happiness multiplies by dividing.

129

Whole Wheat Homemade Noodles

6-7 whole eggs, measuring 1¾ c. 6 c. whole wheat flour
⅓ c. water   dash salt

Beat eggs, add water, and mix well. In a large bowl, measure flour and add egg mixture and salt, stirring with a wooden spoon and then kneading when too stiff to stir until a ball forms. Divide this ball into about 10 portions with a knife. Put portions through the noodle maker until desired thickness and then through the cutter. Spread out to dry.

—*Alice Wilkerson, Fordland, MO*

Quick Drop Noodles

1 egg   ¾ c. whole wheat flour
½ c. milk   dash salt

Beat egg and milk in a large bowl. Add flour and salt. Pour batter on saucer or plate that has a small rim shape (must have a rim or batter will dump out when you do this procedure). Over a large pot of boiling water or soup tip this plate slightly. When batter begins to run over the edge, cut it off with a sharp knife or metal spatula edge. Repeat until batter is gone. After noodles float, cook for 30 seconds longer.

—*Alice Wilkerson, Fordland, MO*

A sorrow shared is but half a trouble,
but a joy shared is a joy made double.

Wash your peas or broccoli; put in pan with a little water. Then add a pinch of soda, or more if you are cooking in a 4- or 6- qt. kettle. Cook slowly and veggies stay green and seem to even taste better. It seems green beans don't retain color as well as broccoli and peas do.

Grating a stick of butter softens it quickly.

Cut down on salt and add good flavors with herbs and spices.

If you have overseasoned your cooking, add a peeled raw potato just before serving.

For drying celery leaves, use young unspotted leaves. Dry them on a screen above stove, then put them on a cookie sheet to make them crisp in the oven, with the oven door open, for about 10 minutes. Crumble them so they are ready to add as a seasoning. Store in tight jars.

Baking soda makes a great scouring powder for bathtubs and vanities.

Use maple syrup instead of sugar in bread recipes. The bread will stay fresh longer, tastes better, and is better for you.

Storing vegetables: Leave your Chinese cabbage in the garden and cover with row cover until ground freezes to stay. Then cut off and trim only what needs to be trimmed and store in ice chest or other almost tight container in cellar.

To store carrots until spring: Wash them clean and cut off greens, then put in crate until just dry. Now put in plastic bread bags and twist shut. Store in cooler in cellar.

NOTES

_____

_____

_____

_____

_____

_____

_____

_____

_____

_____

_____

_____

_____

_____

_____

_____

_____

_____

_____

_____

_____

_____

_____

_____

Cakes

Pear Cake

1½ c. honey
1½ c. olive oil
3 eggs
3 c. whole wheat flour
1 tsp. cinnamon
1 tsp. salt
1 tsp. soda

2 tsp. vanilla
2 c. coconut
1 c. raisins or chopped dates
3 c. raw or canned pears,
    drained and chopped
1 c. pecans, chopped

Cream together honey and oil. Add eggs, one at a time. Add dry ingredients. Mix and add vanilla. Add remaining ingredients and mix until well blended. Pour into a greased and floured bundt pan. Bake at 300°-325° for 1½-2 hours. Cool on rack until cake shrinks from sides of pan. Remove from pan to complete cooling.

—*Mary Showalter, Mt. Solon, VA*

Queen Elizabeth Cake

1 c. boiling water
1 c. dates, chopped
1½ tsp. baking soda
¼ c. butter
½ c. honey
1 egg

1 tsp. vanilla
½ c. walnuts, chopped,
    optional
1½ c. whole wheat flour
1 tsp. baking powder
¼ tsp. salt

First add soda to dates. Pour boiling water over dates and let cool. Cream butter and honey well. Beat in egg, vanilla, and salt. Add dry ingredients alternately with date mixture. Bake at 350° for 1 hour in a square pan.

—*Lillian Mast, Cherry Valley, NY*

Date Spice Cake

1¼ c. water	2 tsp. baking powder
1½ c. dates, chopped	1 tsp. soda
1½ c. prunes, chopped	1 tsp. cinnamon
½ c. butter, softened	¼ tsp. nutmeg
3 eggs	¼ tsp. cloves
¾ c. banana, mashed	1 tsp. vanilla
3 c. (scant) whole grain flour	½ c. nuts, chopped
1¼ tsp. stevia	

Cook water, dates, and prunes together then puree. Cream butter, eggs, and banana together. In a separate bowl, combine the dry ingredients thoroughly. Mix all mixtures together. Stir in vanilla and nuts. Pour into a 9" x 13" pan. Bake at 350° for 28-30 minutes.

Note: Pan size matters. To use a different size, adjust baking time and probably temperature.

—*Mrs. John Houston, Cottage Grove, TN*

Grandma's Cane Molasses Cake

2 c. cream (can be sour) or 1⅓ c. cream and ⅔ c. buttermilk	2 tsp. soda
2 c. molasses	2 tsp. ginger
1 egg	2 tsp. cinnamon
4 c. whole wheat flour	1 tsp. cloves

Beat cream, molasses, and egg until fluffy. Add dry ingredients and mix well. Bake in a greased cake pan at 350° for 30-40 minutes.

—*Eva Troyer, Scottsville, KY*

Silence is one of the most beautiful, impressive, and inspiring things known to men. Don't break it unless you can improve it.

135

Grandma's Spice Marble Cake

1 c. honey or maple syrup	1 Tbsp. molasses
½ c. applesauce	1 tsp. cinnamon
3 eggs	1 tsp. allspice
1½ c. milk	½ tsp. cloves
3 c. wheat flour	½ tsp. nutmeg
3 tsp. baking powder	1 tsp. vanilla
½ tsp. salt	1 tsp. lemon flavoring

Mix together honey and applesauce. Beat and add eggs. Measure flour, baking powder, and salt. Alternate with flour mixture and milk. Divide this batter into 2 parts. To one part add molasses and spices. To the second part add vanilla and lemon flavoring. In a greased baking pan (9" x 13") alternate by spoonful of one then the other. Bake at 350° until toothpick inserted comes out clean.

—*Wilma Schmucker, Mio, MI*

Strawberry Shortcake

4 c. whole wheat flour	½ c. lard or chicken fat
4 tsp. baking powder	2 eggs
½ c. honey	1½ c. milk
¾ tsp. salt	

Cream lard and honey; add rest of ingredients. Mix well. Bake at 350° for 45-60 minutes. Serve warm with fresh strawberries and milk.

—*Mary Nolt, Withee, WI*

Sincerity and truth are the basis of every virtue.

Blueberry Coffee Cake

2 eggs
⅔ c. butter
1 tsp. vanilla
1 Tbsp. honey
2 c. oatmeal
1 c. whole grain flour
1 tsp. salt
2 tsp. soda

½ tsp. cream of tartar
¾ tsp. stevia
2 tsp. baking powder
1 c. buttermilk
3 Tbsp. applesauce
1 c. blueberries
1 c. nuts, chopped

Topping:
3 Tbsp. butter
1 tsp. honey
⅓ c. nuts, chopped

¾ tsp. cinnamon
⅓ c. whole grain flour

Cream together eggs, butter, vanilla, and honey until fluffy. In a separate bowl mix thoroughly oatmeal (which has been ground briefly in blender), flour, salt, soda, cream of tartar, stevia, and baking powder. Add buttermilk and applesauce and mix with egg mixture. Fold in blueberries and nuts. Pour into greased cake pan. Mix together nuts, cinnamon, and flour for topping. Add butter and honey. Sprinkle over top of cake. Bake at 350° for 40-45 minutes.

—*Mrs. John Houston, Cottage Grove, TN*

Happiness Cake

1 c. good thoughts
1 c. kind deeds
1 c. consideration of others

2 c. sacrifice for others
3 c. forgiveness
2 c. well beaten faults

Add tears of joy, sorrow, and sympathy. Fold in 4 c. of faith and prayer. Bake with the heat of human kindness. Serve with a smile. Perfection may never be reached, but it is worth reaching for.

—*Mrs. Junior Detweiler, Redding, IA*

Peach Upside-Down Cake

Topping:	Batter:
¼ c. butter	1 c. whole wheat pastry flour
¼ c. honey	2 tsp. baking powder
1 tsp. cinnamon	⅓ c. maple syrup
¼ tsp. nutmeg	¼ c. oil
2 c. peaches, sliced	1 egg
	3 Tbsp. milk
	1 tsp. vanilla
	1 tsp. lemon peel, finely grated

Place the butter, honey, cinnamon, and nutmeg in a small saucepan. Stir over medium heat until the butter is melted. Pour mixture into bottom of 8" square cake pan. Make an even layer of peaches over the honey-butter mixture. Set the pan aside while you make the batter. Sift together the flour and baking powder. In another bowl, beat together the maple syrup, oil, egg, milk, vanilla, and lemon peel. Stir the flour mixture into the liquid mixture. Beat just enough to mix well; take care not to overbeat. Evenly pour the batter over the peaches. Bake at 350° for 1 hour or until golden brown.

—*Laura Yoder, Free Union, VA*

Cherry Dump Cake

1 pt. sour cherries	½ c. honey
1 c. whole wheat flour	⅔ c. milk
2 tsp. baking powder	2 Tbsp. butter

Melt butter in a 9" square baking pan. In a bowl, mix flour and baking powder with honey and milk. Stir until dry ingredients are moistened and blended. Pour into pan then spread can of cherries and juice evenly over batter. Bake in a 350° oven for 45 minutes.

—*Miss Betty Hilty, Oakfield, ME*

Rhubarb Cake

2 eggs	½ c. applesauce
2 tsp. soda	1 Tbsp. honey
4 c. whole grain flour	2 c. buttermilk or apple juice
2 tsp. salt	2 tsp. vanilla
1¼ tsp. stevia	3 c. rhubarb, diced
½ c. butter	

Beat eggs until fluffy and set aside. Combine dry ingredients thoroughly, then add rest of ingredients. Add eggs last. Sprinkle with crumbs and bake at 350° for 60 minutes.

Crumb Topping:

3 Tbsp. butter	⅓ c. nuts, chopped
¼ c. date sugar or 1 Tbsp. honey	1 tsp. cinnamon
	⅓ c. whole grain flour

Melt butter with sweetener. Add rest of ingredients and mix until crumbly.

—Mrs. John Houston, Cottage Grove, TN

Angel Food Cake

2¼ c. egg whites	½ c. maple syrup
1 tsp. salt	½ c. honey
2 tsp. cream of tartar	1¾ c. sifted spelt flour
2 tsp. vanilla	

Have the eggs at room temperature. Put egg whites, salt, cream of tartar, and vanilla in a bowl and beat until very soft peaks form. Gradually beat in the maple syrup and honey which has been slightly warmed. Continue beating until stiff peaks form. Sift the flour over the beaten egg white mixture in 4 additions and fold in carefully after each addition. Bake in tube pan at 350° for 35-40 minutes.

—Mrs. Reuben Miller, Millersburg, OH

Whole Wheat Angel Food Cake

2 c. egg whites
1¼ tsp. cream of tartar
¼ tsp. salt
1 tsp. vanilla
1 c. honey (may substitute
    maple syrup or sorghum)
1 c. whole wheat flour

1 tsp. baking powder
¼ c. arrowroot powder or
    cornstarch
2 Tbsp. carob powder or flour
1 tsp. cinnamon
¼ tsp. nutmeg

Beat together first 4 ingredients until stiff peaks form. Add honey in 3-4 additions. You may prefer using a scraper to mix in sweetener as it tends to settle to bottom of bowl. Sift together dry ingredients 5 times and add in several additions. Turn batter into angel food tube cake pan. Bake at 350° for approximately 1 hour or until done.

—*Mrs. Urie R. Miller, Shipshewana, IN*

Hawaiian Cake

2 c. wheat flour
2 tsp. soda
1 c. nuts, chopped
¾ c. honey
1 c. unsweetened coconut
1 tsp. vanilla
20 oz. can crushed pineapple
    with juice

Topping:
3-4 oz. cream cheese
½ c. unsweetened coconut
¼ c. butter
½ c. nuts
sweetener (maple syrup or
    honey)

Mix batter ingredients and pour into greased 9" x 13" pan. Bake at 350° for 45 minutes.

—*Mrs. Junior Detweiler, Redding, IA*

Carob Cake

1½ c. whole wheat flour
1 Tbsp. carob powder
1 tsp. soda
½ tsp. salt
1 c. honey

1 Tbsp. vinegar
1 tsp. pure vanilla extract
6 Tbsp. butter, melted, or
   olive oil
1 c. water

Mix all dry ingredients in 10" baking dish. Make 3 depressions; into one pour melted butter or oil, the second vinegar, the third honey. Pour cold water over all and mix with a fork, but do not beat. Bake at 350° for 30 minutes. Cool in pan on rack. Serve right from pan. Delicious with whipped cream sweetened with honey.

—*Mary E. Showalter, Mt. Solon, VA*

Wacky Cake

3 c. whole wheat flour
1 c. honey
⅓ c. carob powder
2 tsp. soda
1 tsp. salt

2 tsp. vanilla
2 Tbsp. vinegar
½ c. olive oil
1¾ c. water

Mix together. Do not beat. Pour into ungreased 11" x 13" pan. Bake at 350° for 35-40 minutes.

Frosting: Mix peanut butter and honey until creamy and spread on cake.

—*Cyndi Davis, Flemingsburg, KY*

Love in action is when the other person's needs become more important than our own.

Apple Cake

3 c. whole wheat flour
1¼ c. sorghum molasses
1 c. thick sour cream
1 tsp. soda
1 tsp. salt

1 Tbsp. vanilla
3 eggs
3 c. apples, diced
1 c. pecans or walnuts

Mix together first 7 ingredients. Beat 3 minutes. Stir in apples and nuts. Spread in 2 8" pans. Bake 1 hour at 350°.

—*Alma Rhodes, Scottsville, KY*

Honey and Apple Cake

1 c. honey
2 c. (scant) applesauce, divided
2 eggs
3 c. spelt flour
1½ tsp. baking soda

¼ tsp. salt
1 tsp. cinnamon
1 c. raisins
½ c. nuts, chopped
⅛ tsp. nutmeg

Cream ½ c. applesauce and honey together. Add eggs, one at a time, beating well. Add dry ingredients alternately with the remaining applesauce. Add nuts and raisins. Bake in a well greased cake pan for 30-40 minutes at 350°.

—*Mrs. Crist Yoder, Baltic, OH*

He that hath pity upon the poor lendeth unto the Lord;
and that which he hath given will pay him again.
—Proverbs 19:17

Applesauce Cake

2 c. whole grain flour	1 c. nuts, chopped
1 tsp. soda	½ c. butter
½ tsp. salt	2 eggs
½ tsp. cloves	1 c. applesauce
½ tsp. nutmeg	1 c. raisins
1 tsp. cinnamon	1½ tsp. vanilla
1¼ tsp. stevia	1 tsp. honey

Combine thoroughly the dry ingredients and nuts. Cream together butter and eggs, then add applesauce, raisins, vanilla, and honey. Mix well. Pour into 8" x 4" pan. Bake at 350° for 40-45 minutes. A double recipe fills a 9" x 13" x 2" pan nicely.

—*Mrs. John Houston, Cottage Grove, TN*

Oatmeal Cake

2½ c. buttermilk	2⅔ c. whole grain flour
2 c. oatmeal	1 tsp. stevia
1 c. butter	2 tsp. soda
2 tsp. vanilla	1 tsp. salt
4 eggs	1 tsp. baking powder
1½ Tbsp. honey	2 tsp. cinnamon

Combine buttermilk and oatmeal and let set 20 minutes. Beat together butter, vanilla, eggs, and honey until fluffy. In a separate bowl, mix the dry ingredients thoroughly. Add the egg mixture, then the buttermilk and oats mixture. Mix well. Bake in a 13" x 9" pan at 350° for 45-50 minutes.

—*Mrs. John Houston, Cottage Grove, TN*

Practice makes perfect, so be careful what you practice.

Oatmeal Cake

2 c. quick oatmeal
1 c. butter
2½ c. boiling water
2½ c. honey
2 tsp. vanilla
4 eggs, beaten

3¾ c. flour
2 tsp. soda
2 tsp. cinnamon
½ tsp. nutmeg
⅛ tsp. salt

Mix oats, butter, and boiling water in a large bowl. Let set 15-20 minutes. Then add honey, vanilla, and eggs. Add other ingredients and pour into greased and floured cake pan. Bake 30-40 minutes in 350° oven. Delicious plain or iced with coconut topping.

—*Lillian Mast, Cherry Valley, NY*

Carrot Cake

3 c. carrots, shredded
2 Tbsp. blackstrap molasses
2 eggs
1 banana, smoothly mashed
⅔ c. oil
3 c. whole wheat or spelt flour
3 Tbsp. (rounded) fine rolled oats

1½ tsp. baking powder
1½ tsp. cinnamon
1½ tsp. vanilla
1 c. nuts, chopped, optional
⅛-¼ tsp. stevia

Steam the carrots for 3 minutes. Cool. Blend carrots, molasses, eggs, banana, and oil. Add rest of ingredients and mix well. If batter is too thick, add a little milk or yogurt. Pour into greased and floured 10" x 13" pan. Bake at 350° for 30 minutes.

Refrigerate whole grain flour or it will spoil.

Carrot Cake

2 c. whole wheat flour	¾ c. oil
2 tsp. baking powder	¾ c. honey
1½ tsp. soda	4 eggs
1 tsp. salt	2 c. carrots, grated
2 tsp. cinnamon	1 c. crushed pineapple or
½ c. nuts, chopped	drained peaches

Mix dry ingredients well. Add oil, honey, and eggs. Mix well; stir in remaining ingredients. Pour into 2 or 3 greased and floured 9" layer pans or a 9" x 13" pan. Bake at 350° for 35-40 minutes. Cool a few minutes in pans then turn out and thoroughly cool on racks. Frost.

Cream Cheese Frosting:

8 oz. cream cheese	2-4 Tbsp. honey
6 Tbsp. butter, softened	1 tsp. vanilla

Beat cream cheese and butter until fluffy. Beat in honey and vanilla.

—*Eva Troyer, Scottsville, KY*

Pumpkin Cake

2 c. pumpkin	2 tsp. soda
½-⅔ pt. sorghum molasses	2 tsp. baking powder
3 eggs	½ tsp. salt
1 c. (scant) plain yogurt	cinnamon, ginger, cloves,
2 c. whole wheat bread flour	or allspice, optional

Whip pumpkin with whisk till smooth. Add sorghum and mix thoroughly. Beat in eggs, one at a time. Whip yogurt till smooth, then slowly add in pumpkin mixture, beating to keep smooth. Mix together dry ingredients and add to wet ingredients. Mix well. Pour into a 9" x 13" greased cake pan. Bake at 350° for 30-45 minutes.

—*Alma Rhodes, Scottsville, KY*

Banana Topsy-Turvy Cake

Topping:

3 Tbsp. butter	8 oz. can unsweetened
¼ c. honey	pineapple slices, drained
½ c. walnuts, chopped	

Melt butter in a 9" square baking dish; pour honey over butter and arrange pineapple slices and nuts on top.

Cake:

½ c. butter	1 tsp. soda
1 c. honey	½ tsp. baking powder
2 eggs	½ tsp. salt
1 tsp. vanilla	1 c. rolled oats
1¼ c. whole wheat flour	½ c. bananas, mashed
¾ c. buttermilk	

Beat together butter and honey until light and fluffy. Blend in eggs and vanilla. Add combined flour, soda, baking powder, and salt to the batter mixture alternately with buttermilk. Mix well after each addition. Stir in oats and bananas. Pour over topping. Bake in preheated oven at 350° for 45-50 minutes. Loosen side of cake pan; immediately invert on serving plate. Serve warm or cold with whipped cream.

—Mary E. Showalter, Mt. Solon, VA

Many great ideas have been lost because the people who had them couldn't handle being laughed at.

Banana Cake

1 tsp. cinnamon	½ c. butter, softened
1 tsp. soda	1 c. banana, mashed
1¼ tsp. stevia	2 eggs
2 c. whole grain flour	1 c. milk
1½ tsp. baking powder	1 tsp. vanilla

Combine dry ingredients thoroughly. Cream butter, banana, and eggs. Mix to dry ingredients. Add milk and vanilla, beating well. Pour into an 8" x 12" pan. Bake at 350° for 30 minutes.

—*Mrs. John Houston, Cottage Grove, TN*

Banana Chip Cake

⅔ c. maple syrup or honey	2 c. whole wheat flour
½ c. oil	1 tsp. soda
egg replacer* or 2 eggs	½ c. carob chips
3 ripe bananas, mashed	

Mix all together. Do not overmix. Pour into an 8" pan and bake at 350° for 30-40 minutes. 2½ c. oat or spelt flour may be used instead of wheat.

* Egg replacer = ½ c. finely ground flaxseed mixed with 1½ c. water. Refrigerate one hour before using. ½ c. = 2 eggs.

Variation: Use 1½ c. applesauce instead of bananas and carob chips. Can also be baked as bars.

—*Mrs. David Weaver, Millersburg, OH*

Some stevia-sweetened cakes improve
in flavor after standing overnight.

Approximate Stevia Sweetness Equivalents

⅓-½ tsp. white extract powder .... 1 c. sugar

1 tsp. Stevia Clear Liquid .... 1 c. sugar

1 Tbsp. whole leaf dark liquid concentrate.. 1 c. sugar

1½-2 Tbsp. Honey Leaf powder .... 1 c. sugar

1½-2 Tbsp. Stevia Plus powder .... 1 c. sugar

18-24 Stevia Plus packets............................ 1 c. sugar

2 tsp. whole leaf dark liquid concentrate..... 1 c. brown sugar

Too much stevia may taste bitter.

When substituting stevia for sugar in your own recipes you may have to adjust for the bulk. Try adding applesauce, apple butter, or plain yogurt.

If you are not used to using stevia, use only about half the amount the recipe calls for. Gradually use more as your taste buds adjust.

On a Diet?
Cut out those nice little dinners for two,
unless there's someone with you.

Frostings, Fillings, & Sauces

Butter Cream Frosting

3 Tbsp. (slightly rounded)   1 c. milk
   cornstarch   ⅓-½ c. butter
⅓-½ c. maple syrup   1 tsp. vanilla

Blend together and boil cornstarch, maple syrup, and milk, stirring constantly until very thick. Cool. Cream together butter and vanilla. Add to cooled mixture. Beat at high speed until fluffy.

Variation: Add crushed pineapple for Pineapple Butter Cream Frosting.

—Erma Hoover, Penn Yan, NY

Icing for Cake

Boil ¾ c. honey, ½ c. butter, and ½ c. cream. After it has boiled down a little (slowly, as it burns), add 1 Tbsp. cornstarch dissolved in ¼ c. milk. Cook cornstarch in, then remove from heat. Cool. If it's too stiff, add some cream. Spread on a cooled cake.

—Laura Royer, Camden, IN

Cream Cheese Icing

8 oz. cream cheese   ¼ c. honey
¼ c. butter   1 tsp. vanilla

Cream all together. If you like a thinner consistency, add a little milk.

—Laura Yoder, Free Union, VA

Coconut Topping

1⅓ c. flaked coconut   ¼ c. cream
¼ c. honey   1 tsp. vanilla
¼ c. butter

Mix together and spread on cake. Broil in hot oven.

—*Lillian Mast, Cherry Valley, NY*

Boiled Honey Frosting

1½ c. honey   2 egg whites, beaten stiff
⅛ tsp. salt

Mix salt with honey in a saucepan. Heat to 238° or until mixture
will spin a thread or make a soft ball when dropped into ice water. Pour hot honey in a thin stream over stiffly beaten egg whites,
beating constantly. Beat till frosting stands in peaks. Spread between layers and over cake. This frosting has a strong honey flavor
similar to the darker-colored honeys, even if you start with light-
colored honey.

—*Elizabeth Mullet, Pantego, NC*

Honey Icing

¼ c. butter, softened   coconut
½ c. honey   nuts or seeds

Blend together and spread over cake.

—*Mrs. Urie R. Miller, Shipshewana, IN*

Frosting for Carrot Cake

3 Tbsp. arrowroot powder	4 oz. cream cheese
¼ tsp. stevia	1 tsp. vanilla
1 c. water or pineapple juice	½ c. unsweetened coconut
¼ c. butter	½ c. pineapple, drained

Mix stevia and arrowroot thoroughly. Add water or juice and cook until thick. Cool and add rest of ingredients. Whip for 5 minutes or until fluffy.

—Mrs. John Houston, Cottage Grove, TN

Maple Syrup Frosting

½ c. maple syrup	¼ c. maple syrup
¾ c. water	2 Tbsp. butter
3 Tbsp. cornstarch	1 tsp. vanilla

Cook ½ c. maple syrup and water until boiling, then add cornstarch mixed with ¼ c. maple syrup. Cook until boiling again, keeping well stirred, until mixture has thickened. Take off from heat and add butter and vanilla. Spread on cake before it cools off.

—Jolene Bontrager, Hillsboro, WI

Carob Brownie Icing

4 Tbsp. butter, melted	⅓ c. honey
2 tsp. vanilla	¼ c. sifted carob

Mix all ingredients and beat till smooth. Can be placed on hot brownies. Also can be used as a carob syrup.

—Loveda Bear, Patriot, OH

Cream Filling

1 pt. milk
1 egg, beaten
½ c. honey
3 Tbsp. cornstarch

2 Tbsp. butter
1 tsp. orange flavoring (or
    any flavoring)

Cook until thick. Cool and spread between layers of cake, or use for icing on top of it. This is good for a creamy cake topping.

—*Laura Royer, Camden, IN*

Chocolate Cream Filling

1 pt. milk
1 egg, beaten
½ c. honey

2 Tbsp. cornstarch
¼ c. cocoa
2 Tbsp. butter

Cook until thick. (Always mix the cornstarch with a bit of the milk before adding it to the mixture.) Cool and spread between layers or on top of a cake.

—*Laura Royer, Camden, IN*

Delicious Date Filling

⅔ c. cream
⅔ c. honey
2 egg yolks
½ c. dates, chopped

½ tsp. vanilla
½ c. almonds, chopped
    and toasted

Mix first four ingredients. Cook over low heat until slightly thickened, stirring constantly (6-7 minutes). Remove from heat; add vanilla and nuts. Cook until thick enough to spread. Enough to fill and cover top of two 8" or 9" layers.

—*Laura Royer, Camden, IN*

Chocolate Fudge Sauce

½ c. cocoa or carob	⅓ c. butter
½ c. honey	1 tsp. vanilla
⅓ c. heavy cream	¼ c. milk
⅓ c. water	1 Tbsp. cornstarch

Mix cocoa, honey, cream, and water together. Cook over medium heat, stirring constantly, until syrup comes to a boil. Boil for 1 minute while stirring. Have cornstarch dissolved in milk. Add it to the boiling sauce while stirring all the while and stir and cook 2 more minutes. Remove from heat. Add butter and vanilla. Beat until glossy and creamy. May be used for chocolate icing. Yield: 1½ c.

—*Laura Royer, Camden, IN*

Pineapple Sauce

1 qt. applesauce	1 can pineapple

Mix together and serve. Can use more applesauce if desired.

—*Iva Kauffman, Monroe, WI*

Pancake Syrup

1 c. honey	1 tsp. maple flavoring,
1 c. sorghum	optional
¾ c. water	1 tsp. vanilla

Mix together and bring to a boil. Boil hard for 2 minutes.

—*Mary Eicher, Quincy, MI*

> *As a jewel of gold in a swine's snout, so is a*
> *fair woman which is without discretion.*
>
> —*Proverbs 11:22*

Cookies & Bars

Wholesome Sweeteners

What is the white granulated sugar we buy at the grocery store? How is it made? Sugar is what is left over from sugar cane or sugar beets after they are chemically processed and highly refined.

Whole natural foods are always a combination of nutrients, vitamins, and minerals. Sugar cane and sugar beets are food, and their dehydrated juices are food.

By the time we buy our sugar at the store, however, it has been so refined that our body does not recognize it as food. While we tend to think brown sugar, raw sugar, and turbinado are better for us, they too are usually just refined sugar with enough molasses added to give them the desired color.

Fructose and high fructose corn syrup are also highly refined sweeteners that are known to unbalance the blood sugar level in our bodies.

Artificial sweeteners such as Equal® and Nutra-Sweet® contain aspartame, which is a toxic substance that has been associated with many health problems, including depression, birth defects, pancreatitis, and seizures.

When we eat refined sugars, we are eating empty, unbalanced calories. In order for our body to balance and detoxify, and to digest this sugar, it has to use up our reserves of insulin, enzymes, vitamins, and minerals.

When we use refined sugars for many years our reserves are depleted and our body will need to borrow these nutrients from deep in our bones, teeth, and vital organs. This is our body's way to try to correct the sugar imbalance. Weakness, decay of teeth, disease, and lowered immunity to sickness can soon follow. Diabetes, candida (yeast), food allergies, headaches, hypoglycemia, weak adrenal glands, mental illness, and chronic fatigue syndrome are just some of the illnesses that can come from eating too much sugar.

The good news is that we do have a choice. We do not have to decide that since regular, refined sugar is so bad for us we will just have to stay away from sweets. There are all-natural sweeteners available that contain many nutrients. Natural sweeteners, too, should be used in moderation, because even they can cause blood sugar imbalances if they are used in excess. Here is a list of a few all-natural sugars:

Honey – Pure, raw honey is full of nutrients and digestive enzymes. Heating honey to over 117° causes it to lose some of its enzymes, but the nutrients will still be there. Babies do not have enough stomach acid to take care of possible bacteria in honey, so be sure not to give raw honey to children under one year of age.

Maple Syrup – This evaporated sap of the sugar maple tree is rich in minerals. It gives a naturally wonderful maple flavor to baked goods and other desserts.

Sorghum – This syrup is made by boiling sorghum cane juice. It contains B vitamins and minerals like calcium and iron. It is delicious in molasses cookies.

Sucanat – Made by dehydrating cane sugar juice, sucanat has great flavor and is rich in minerals. It is probably the easiest to exchange in recipes calling for sugar.

Stevia – A super-sweet herb, stevia is tolerated much better by diabetics than some other natural sweeteners. The biggest problem is adding too much, which produces an unpleasant flavor.

Western medicine will one day admit what has been known in the Orient for years. Sugar is the greatest evil that modern industrial civilization has visited upon the countries of the Far East and Africa.

—Sakurazawa

Applesauce Cookies

1 c. honey	½ tsp. soda
½ c. oil	½ tsp. baking powder
2 eggs, beaten	1 tsp. cinnamon
1 c. applesauce	½ tsp. vanilla
2½ c. whole wheat flour	1 c. sunflower seeds

Stir honey and oil until creamy. Add eggs and applesauce. Sift flour, soda, baking powder, and cinnamon together and add to first mixture. Mix vanilla and sunflower seeds and add. Drop by teaspoon onto a greased cookie sheet. Bake at 375° for 10 minutes.

—*Erma Hoover, Penn Yan, NY*

Applesauce Cookies

2 c. applesauce	½ tsp. cloves
1 c. butter	¼ tsp. salt
2 eggs	1 tsp. nutmeg
1 Tbsp. honey	2½ tsp. soda
4 c. oat bran	1 c. nuts, chopped
2 c. whole grain flour	1 tsp. stevia
2 tsp. cinnamon	

Cream applesauce, butter, eggs, and honey until fluffy. In a separate bowl, mix dry ingredients and nuts thoroughly. Add wet ingredients and mix well. Drop by teaspoonsful on cookie sheet. Flatten. Bake at 375° for 10-12 minutes.

Note: Place cookies on top rack in oven to bake for best results.

—*Mrs. John Houston, Cottage Grove, TN*

Pumpkin Cookies

1½ c. lard

1 c. molasses or ¾ c. honey

3 eggs

3 c. cooked pumpkin, mashed

1 Tbsp. vanilla

6 c. flour

1 Tbsp. baking powder

1 Tbsp. soda

1 tsp. salt

1½ c. raisins, optional

½ c. nuts, optional

Cream together lard and molasses. Add rest of ingredients and mix well. Bake at 350° for 10-12 minutes.

—*Mary Nolt, Withee, WI*

Whole Wheat Apple Cookies

1 c. butter

1 c. honey

2 eggs

2 c. apples, finely diced

1 c. nuts, chopped

1 c. milk

2 tsp. cinnamon

2 tsp. soda

1 tsp. salt

2 tsp. vanilla

4 c. whole wheat flour

2 c. raisins

Cream butter and honey. Add eggs and vanilla then dry ingredients and milk. Stir in apples, nuts, and raisins. Bake at 350° for 10-15 minutes.

—*Mrs. Amos Fisher, Jersey Shore, PA*

Freedom is not the right to do as you please,

but the liberty to do as you ought.

Banana Chip Cookies

2½ c. whole grain flour   ½ c. butter
½ tsp. salt   ¾ c. honey
½ tsp. nutmeg   1 egg
½ tsp. cinnamon   1 tsp. vinegar
¼ tsp. cloves   2½ tsp. soda
¾ c. carob chips   ½ c. nuts
1 c. ripe bananas, mashed

Mix together first 5 ingredients. In a large bowl, cream butter and honey. Beat until light and fluffy; add egg, bananas, soda, and vinegar. Beat until fluffy. Gradually add flour mixture, mixing well. Stir in chips and nuts. Bake 10-15 minutes at 350°.

—*Lillian Mast, Cherry Valley, NY*

Honey Raisin Cookies

½ c. olive oil   ½ tsp. baking powder
⅓ c. honey   ¼ tsp. soda
2 eggs   ¼ tsp. salt
1¼ c. whole wheat flour   ⅔ c. raisins
½ tsp. nutmeg   ¼ tsp. pure vanilla extract

Cream olive oil and honey thoroughly. Add the eggs; beat until well mixed. Mix together the flour, nutmeg, baking powder, soda, and salt. Add the creamed mixture; stir until mixed. Add raisins and vanilla. Drop batter by tablespoonsful on a greased cookie sheet, 2" apart. Bake at 350° for 12 minutes or until golden brown. Yield: 2 dozen.

—*Mary E. Showalter, Mt. Solon, VA*

160

Raisin Drop Cookies

¾ c. raisins
¾ c. water
1 c. whole wheat flour
1 tsp. cinnamon
½ tsp. nutmeg
¼ tsp. salt
1¼ tsp. stevia
¼ c. nuts, chopped

1 tsp. soda
5 Tbsp. butter
¼ c. applesauce
2 tsp. vanilla
¼ c. milk
2 c. rolled oats, chopped
coarsely in blender

Cook raisins and water 5 minutes. In a large bowl, combine thoroughly the dry ingredients and nuts. Mix butter, applesauce, vanilla, and milk and add to dry ingredients and nuts. Add oats. Add cooked raisins last (with the water). Let set 15 minutes. Drop by teaspoon on cookie sheets. Bake in a 350° oven for 10-15 minutes till lightly browned.

—*Mrs. John Houston, Cottage Grove, TN*

Healthy Oat and Raisin Cookies

1 c. whole wheat flour
1 tsp. soda
½ tsp. Real salt
2 c. quick oats
¼ c. wheat germ
¾ c. butter

1 c. honey
2 eggs
1 tsp. vanilla
¾ c. coconut
¾ c. raisins
½ c. nuts, optional

Combine dry ingredients. Cream butter, honey, eggs, and vanilla. Add dry ingredients and mix well. Add coconut, raisins, and nuts. Bake at 350° for 10-12 minutes.

—*Mrs. David J. Yoder, Clare, MI*

Health Rounds

1 c. butter or ¾ c. oil
1 c. honey
2 eggs, beaten
½ tsp. salt
2 tsp. vanilla
1 tsp. baking powder

3 c. whole wheat flour
1 c. rolled oats
1 c. sunflower seeds
1½ c. nuts, chopped
2 c. raisins

Cream butter or oil and honey. Add eggs, salt, and vanilla. Blend in dry ingredients. Stir in seeds, nuts, and raisins. Drop by teaspoonsful onto an ungreased cookie sheet. Bake 10-12 minutes at 375°.

—*Loveda Martin, Finger, TN*

Honey Drop Cookies

¾ c. honey
½ c. butter
2 eggs, well beaten
1 c. raisins
½ c. walnuts, chopped
2 c. whole wheat flour

½ tsp. baking powder
1 tsp. soda
¼ tsp. sea salt
½ tsp. cinnamon
½ tsp. ground cloves

Mix honey, butter, and eggs well. Add raisins and walnuts. Sift flour, baking powder, soda, and salt together and add to honey mixture a little at a time. Add spices; blend well. Drop by teaspoonsful onto a greased baking sheet. Bake in a preheated 370° oven for 12-15 minutes. Yield: 4 dozen.

—*Mary S. Yoder, Wooster, OH*

Work is the best way invented to kill time.

Oatmeal Molasses Cookies

1 c. butter	½ tsp. salt
2 c. sorghum	2 tsp. cinnamon
2 eggs	1 tsp. nutmeg
2½ c. whole wheat flour	5 c. rolled oats
4 tsp. baking powder	2 c. raisins
4 tsp. soda	

Melt together butter and sorghum; add eggs. Sift together dry ingredients and add. Stir in oats and raisins. Drop by teaspoon on cookie sheet. Bake at 350° for 12-15 minutes.

—*Mrs. Urie R. Miller, Shipshewana, IN*

Sunflower Seed Cookies

1 c. butter	1½ c. whole wheat pastry
1 c. honey or sorghum	flour
2 eggs	1 tsp. soda
1 tsp. vanilla	3 c. oatmeal
½ tsp. salt	1 c. sunflower seeds or coconut

Mix all together in order given. Bake at 375° till golden brown.

—*Mrs. Esther Yoder, Hillsboro, WI*

God often comforts us, not by changing the circumstances of our lives, but by changing our attitudes toward them.

Debbie Cookies

1 c. butter	½ tsp. nutmeg
4 eggs	1½ tsp. soda
½ c. applesauce	2 c. whole grain flour
1½ Tbsp. honey	4 c. oats
2 tsp. vanilla	2 c. oat bran
2 tsp. cinnamon	1¼ tsp. stevia
1 tsp. salt	

Cream butter and eggs until fluffy. Add applesauce, honey, and vanilla and beat well. In a separate bowl, combine dry ingredients thoroughly and add to wet ingredients; beat well. Let set in refrigerator overnight. Shape into flat round cookies. Bake at 375° for 12 minutes.

Tip: Store cookies as soon as they are cooled for best results.

Frosting:

5 Tbsp. flour	1 c. butter
1 tsp. stevia	½ c. cream cheese
1 c. apple juice, water, or milk	1 tsp. vanilla

Cook flour, stevia, and apple juice until thick. Cool thoroughly. Beat butter, cream cheese, and vanilla, then add flour mixture. Beat 5 minutes till very fluffy.

—*Mrs. John Houston, Cottage Grove, TN*

Serenity is not freedom from the storm, but peace amid the storm.

Whole Wheat Carob Chip Cookies

1 c. butter	½ c. raisins
2 eggs	2 (6 oz.) pkg. carob chips
½ c. honey	2 c. oatmeal
1 tsp. water	½ c. peanut butter
1½ c. whole wheat flour	1 tsp. vanilla
1 tsp. baking soda	

Beat butter, honey, eggs, and water until fluffy, then sift in flour and baking soda. Mix well and add rest of ingredients. Mix well. Drop by teaspoonsful onto cookie sheets and bake at 375° for 10 minutes.

—Mrs. Naomi Ruth Bontrager, Mio, MI

Natural Tollhouse Cookies

1 c. butter	2 c. whole wheat flour
½ c. honey	2 c. carob chips
2 eggs	½ c. nuts
1 tsp. vanilla	½ c. unsweetened coconut
1 tsp. soda	½ c. quick oats
1 tsp. salt	

Cream together butter and honey. Beat in eggs and vanilla. Sift together soda, salt, and flour and add to butter mixture. Fold in rest of ingredients. Drop by tablespoon onto greased cookie sheets. Bake at 350° for 12-15 minutes.

—Mrs. David J. Yoder, Clare, MI

> *When I'm right, no one remembers.*
> *When I'm wrong, no one forgets.*

Fruity Cookies

3 bananas	½ tsp. salt
1 c. dates, chopped	2 c. rolled oats
⅓ c. oil	1 tsp. vanilla

Preheat oven to 350°. Grease cookie sheet. Mash bananas. Add dates and oil; mix with a fork. Add remaining ingredients and let stand a few minutes for oats to absorb moisture. Drop by teaspoonful on cookie sheet. Bake 25 minutes or until nicely browned. Cool before removing from cookie sheet.

Variation: Add cinnamon, nutmeg, or allspice.

—Laura Yoder, Free Union, VA

Peanut Butter Oatmeal Cookies

2 eggs	1 c. pure peanut butter
½ c. honey	3 c. quick oats
½ tsp. vanilla	1½ tsp. soda
⅓ c. butter	1 Tbsp. sour milk

Mix soda and sour milk. Beat eggs, add honey, vanilla, butter, and peanut butter, and mix well. Add oats and soda. Stir all together. Drop and flatten. Bake at 350° for 10 minutes or until light brown.

—Irene Mae Yoder, Oakland, MD

> *It is good for me that I have been afflicted;*
> *that I might learn thy statutes.*
> *—Psalms 119:71*

Peanut Butter Cookies

6 Tbsp. butter, softened	½ c. water
½ c. natural peanut butter (room temperature)	2 c. + 2 Tbsp. whole wheat flour
2 eggs	2 tsp. stevia
1½ tsp. vanilla	1 tsp. baking powder
1 tsp. honey	1¾ c. unsweetened coconut

Beat first six ingredients together until creamy. Combine dry ingredients thoroughly and add to creamed mixture. Mix well. Mixture will be stiff. Drop by teaspoonful onto cookie sheet. Flatten with fork. Bake at 350° for 9-10 minutes. Allow to cool 2 minutes before removing from pans.

—Mrs. John Houston, Cottage Grove, TN

Delicious Sorghum Cookies

1 qt. lard or butter	1 Tbsp. salt
2 qt. sorghum	2 lb. raisins
½ c. (scant) soda	6 lb. whole wheat pastry flour (or more to make a very stiff dough)
1 c. buttermilk or sour milk	
2 Tbsp. cinnamon	
2 Tbsp. nutmeg	1 qt. nuts, chopped, optional

Mix all together. Roll dough into balls and flatten on cookie sheet. Bake at 350° until nice and brown, but not burnt. Yield:150-200 cookies.

—Mrs. Esther Yoder, Hillsboro, WI

> *A wise man's heart guides his mouth.*
> *—Proverbs 16:23*

Molasses Cookies

¾ c. butter

1 egg

¼ c. molasses

2 c. flour

½ tsp. stevia

2 tsp. soda

1 tsp. cinnamon

½ tsp. cloves

½ tsp. ginger

½ tsp. salt

Cream butter, egg, and molasses until fluffy. In a separate bowl, mix dry ingredients thoroughly. Add butter mixture and mix well. Drop by teaspoonsful on cookie sheets. Flatten. Bake at 375° for 10-12 minutes.

—Mrs. John Houston, Cottage Grove, TN

Honey Ginger Snaps

¾ c. unsalted butter

¾ c. honey

¼ c. molasses

1 egg

1 tsp. vanilla

¼ c. fresh ginger, finely grated

2½ c. whole wheat flour

1 Tbsp. ground ginger

2 tsp. soda

½ tsp. sea salt

Mix ingredients in order given and drop on cookie sheets. Bake at 350° for 12-15 minutes.

—Mrs. Leroy B. Miller, Middlefield, OH

Sugarfree cookies do not tend to change much in appearance as they bake. So it is important always to flatten them.

Maple Granola Cookies

3 eggs, beaten
1 c. honey
1 c. oil
1½ tsp. vanilla
1 tsp. maple flavoring

1½ tsp. Real salt
1¼ tsp. baking soda
3¾ c. granola
3½ c. whole wheat flour

Combine all the ingredients except flour and granola. Mix well. Add the rest of the ingredients. Drop by teaspoon on greased cookie sheets. Bake at 325° for 10-12 minutes.

—Mrs. David J. Yoder, Clare, MI

Nut Frosties

¼ c. butter
⅓ c. honey
1 egg
1 tsp. vanilla

2 c. whole wheat flour
¾ tsp. soda
1 Tbsp. sour cream

Mix soda with sour cream. Beat egg, butter, and honey. Add rest of ingredients and mix well. Shape dough into 1" balls. Place on cookie sheet and make a depression in center of each cookie. Fill with filling made of:

1 c. walnuts or pecans,
    chopped
1 Tbsp. maple syrup

¼ c. sour cream
add vinegar to sour
    cream, optional

Bake at 350° for 10 minutes or until lightly browned.

—Irene Mae Yoder, Oakland, MD

Tropical Cookies

½ c. butter, melted   2 c. whole grain flour
½ c. orange juice concentrate   ¼ c. oat bran
1 c. coconut, shredded   ½ tsp. soda
1 c. crushed pineapple with juice

Combine ingredients in order given. Bake at 350° for 20 minutes. Yield: 3 dozen.

—*Emma Hoover, Bluff Point, NY*

Sugarfree Cookies

½ c. apples, chopped   ½ tsp. salt
½ c. dates, chopped   1⅓ c. whole wheat flour
1 c. raisins   1 tsp. vanilla
1 c. water   1 tsp. soda
⅓ c. oil   1 tsp. cinnamon
3 eggs   ½ c. walnuts, chopped

Cook together apples, dates, raisins, and water for 3 minutes. Cool. Add remaining ingredients and mix well. Drop on greased cookie sheet. Bake at 350° for 15 minutes. Do not overbake.

—*Mrs. Junior Detweiler, Redding, IA*

A Recipe for a Good Home
Combine a taste of comfort with a generous lot of caring. Sprinkle with some good times and a lot of love and sharing.

Thumbprints

½ c. butter
½ c. honey
2 eggs
2 tsp. vanilla
3 c. whole wheat flour

Filling:
15 oz. crushed pineapple
3 c. dates, chopped
¼ c. water
1 tsp. vanilla

Cream butter and honey. Beat in eggs and vanilla. Stir in flour. Chill about 2 hours. Preheat oven to 325°. Roll dough into balls, place on cookie sheet, make a thumb imprint in the middle of each one, and fill with date filling. Bake 15 minutes or until done.

Filling: Combine all ingredients and cook until thick.

—*Sharon Troyer, Millersburg, OH*

No-Bake Carob Wisps

½-¾ c. honey
½ c. carob powder
1 tsp. vanilla extract
½ c. milk

¼ tsp. salt
½ c. butter
2½ c. rolled oatmeal

Combine honey, carob, vanilla, milk, salt, and butter in a small, heavy saucepan. Bring to a boil over medium heat and boil approximately 5 minutes, stirring constantly. Remove from heat. Stir in oatmeal. Drop by teaspoon onto waxed paper. Allow to cool. Chill or freeze if desired.

Note: This is an extremely versatile recipe. Experiment! Try replacing some of the oatmeal with unsweetened dried coconut or granola. Add nutmeats if you like or raisins, etc...

—*Charlene Kennell, South Wayne, WI*

Carob Frosted Cookies

Cookies:
½ c. butter
½ c. oil
½ c. warm honey
2 egg yolks
1¾ c. whole wheat flour
¼ tsp. salt

Frosting:
1 c. carob powder
1 c. water
2 Tbsp. honey
2 Tbsp. butter

Mix together butter, oil, honey, and egg yolks until smooth. Add flour and salt. Pat evenly into greased 11" x 14" pan. Bake at 350° for 20 minutes or until firm. While still hot put on the frosting. Cut into bars.

Frosting: Bring to a boil in saucepan the carob powder and water. Cook slowly on very low heat for 5-8 minutes. Cool and add honey and butter.

—Mrs. Leroy Auker, Elk Horn, KY

Whoopie Pie Cookies

1 c. butter
1⅓ c. sorghum
2 eggs
2 tsp. vanilla
1 c. sour milk
1 c. hot water

4 c. whole wheat flour,
   sifted
1 c. carob
2 tsp. salt
2 tsp. soda
2 tsp. cinnamon

Cream together butter, sorghum, eggs, and vanilla. Sift together dry ingredients and add alternately with sour milk and hot water. Drop by teaspoon onto cookie sheet. Bake at 350° for 8-10 minutes. Cool. Spread half of cookies with sorghum or honey if desired, then with peanut butter; top with another cookie to form a sandwich. Or use filling of your choice. Store in a cool place.

—Mrs. Urie R. Miller, Shipshewana, IN

Oatmeal Granola Bars

5 c. Prairie Gold® flour	3 eggs
3 c. oatmeal	1⅔ c. lard
4½ c. granola	2½ c. honey
1 Tbsp. soda	2½ c. yogurt
1 tsp. salt	2 tsp. vanilla
2 Tbsp. cinnamon	½ c. coconut

Mix dry ingredients except for coconut well. Beat eggs, lard, honey, yogurt, and vanilla together and add to dry ingredients. Blend and spread into greased pans. Sprinkle coconut on top. Bake at 350° for 15-20 minutes.

—*Mrs. Ervin Bontrager, Hillsboro, WI*

Great Granola Bars

3½ c. quick oats	⅓ c. honey
½ c. unsweetened coconut	⅓ c. cane molasses
¾ c. walnuts or almonds, chopped	1 egg
1 c. dates, chopped	½ tsp. cinnamon
1 c. butter	1 tsp. vanilla
	½ tsp. salt

Melt butter; remove from heat; stir in honey, vanilla, and molasses. Add egg to dry ingredients, then add butter mixture. Mix well and press in a 9" x 13" pan. Bake at 350° for 20 minutes. Cut when cool and remove when completely cooled.

—*Ada Miller, Hazleton, IA*

So, whether you eat or drink; or whatever
you do, do all to the glory of God.
—*I Corinthians 10:31*

173

Granola Bars

5 c. old-fashioned oats	¾ c. almonds, ground
¾ c. wheat germ	1 c. dried pineapples, diced
½ c. bran	½ c. apple pieces
½ c. sesame seeds	5 c. granola
¾ c. coconut	1½ c. prunes, chopped
½ c. almonds	2 c. pecans, chopped
¾ c. flaxseed	1 c. pumpkin seeds
2-3 c. brown rice syrup	4 c. dates
⅓ c. fresh apple juice	3 c. water

Chop dates in blender with the water. Mix all together and press into pans for bars. For cookies mix all together in food processor; roll into balls; then roll in fine coconut. Refrigerate

—Mrs. David Weaver, Millersburg, OH

Pumpkin Bars

½ c. olive oil	2 c. whole wheat flour
1 c. honey	1 tsp. soda
4 eggs	2 c. pumpkin
2 tsp. baking powder	2 tsp. cinnamon

Mix all ingredients together and put in greased jelly roll pan. Bake at 350° for 20-25 minutes. Frost with your favorite frosting if desired.

—Jolene Bontrager, Hillsboro, WI

For a sweeter finished product in recipes asking for apple juice, you can use the frozen concentrate instead of the juice.

Pumpkin Pie Squares

1 c. spelt flour
½ c. rolled oats
½ tsp. stevia
½ c. olive oil
3 c. milk
2 c. pumpkin, mashed
4 eggs

1 tsp. stevia
2 tsp. cinnamon
1 tsp. salt
1 tsp. ginger
1 tsp. cloves
¾ c. nuts, chopped

Combine flour, oats, ½ tsp. stevia, and oil and press into 9" x 13" pan. Beat the rest of the ingredients except nuts and pour over crust. Sprinkle with nuts. Bake at 350° for 20 minutes or until almost set.

—*Laura Yoder, Free Union, VA*

Zucchini Bars

1 c. honey or grape concentrate
½ c. oil or butter
3 eggs
2 c. wheat flour
2 c. zucchini, grated

1 tsp. soda
1 tsp. baking powder
¾ c. quick oats
1 c. nuts, chopped

Preheat oven to 350°. Mix in order given. Beat well and pour into 15" x 10" pan and bake 15-20 minutes or until golden.

—*Mrs. Junior Detweiler, Redding, IA*

Blessed is she whose daily tasks are a work of love; for her willing hands and happy heart transform duty into joyous service to all her family and God.

Carob Brownies

2 eggs
⅔ c. honey
½ c. butter, melted
1 tsp. vanilla
1 banana
½ tsp. salt

1 tsp. soda
¾ c. water
⅓ c. carob, sifted
1 c. whole wheat flour
1 c. broken walnut pieces

Beat eggs slightly; add honey, cooled butter, vanilla, and banana. Mix well. Add dry ingredients alternately with water. Then add walnut pieces. Butter and flour a 13" x 9" glass baking dish and bake exactly 23 minutes at 350°.

—*Loveda Bear, Patriot, OH*

Peanut Butter Swirl Bars

½ c. butter
1 c. maple syrup
1 egg
½ c. peanut butter
1 tsp. vanilla

1 c. whole wheat flour
½ tsp. salt
¼ tsp. baking powder
1 c. oatmeal

Cream first 5 ingredients together. Combine dry ingredients and add to creamed mixture. Spread into greased 9" x 13" pan. Bake at 350° for 25 minutes.

—*Mrs. Johnny Miller, Loudonville, OH*

O Lord, help my words to be gracious and tender today,

for tomorrow I may have to eat them.

Oatmeal Date Squares

½ c. hot water
1½ c. dates, cut
½ c. sorghum
½ tsp. salt
2 Tbsp. lemon juice
2 Tbsp. clear jel
¼ c. water

Crumbs:
½ c. butter, softened
1½ c. whole wheat flour
1¾ c. oatmeal
1 tsp. soda
½ tsp. salt
½-¾ c. sorghum (just
enough so it crumbles easily)

Put half of crumbs in a 9" x 13" pan. Pour in filling, then crumble rest of crumbs on top of filling. Pat in lightly. Bake in 350° oven until lightly browned. Cut in squares when cool.

—*Mrs. J.T., Hestand, KY*

Davy Crockett Bars

¾ c. butter
2 tsp. vanilla
1 c. applesauce
3 eggs
1 Tbsp. honey
2 c. oatmeal
1¾ c. whole grain flour
½ c. water

1¼ tsp. stevia
1 tsp. salt
1 c. unsweetened coconut
1 tsp. soda
1 tsp. baking powder
1½ c. chopped nuts
1 c. raisins

Cream butter, vanilla, applesauce, eggs, and honey until fluffy. In a separate bowl combine dry ingredients and nuts and mix thoroughly. Add to applesauce mixture. Cook raisins in water and mix with rest of ingredients. Spread in 9" x 13" cookie sheet. Bake 10-15 min. at 350°. Do not overbake!
This is one of our favorites.

—*Mrs. John Houston, Cottage Grove, IN*

Walnut Brownies

½ c. butter
½ c. carob powder
½ c. oil
1 c. honey
2 eggs

1 tsp. vanilla
½ c. nuts
1¼ c. wheat flour
½ tsp. soda
½ tsp. baking powder

Melt butter; add carob powder and oil. Remove from heat and add honey. Stir. Cool. Beat eggs and vanilla; add to butter mixture. Add soda, baking powder, and nuts. Stir in flour and spread mixture in a greased 9" x 13" pan. Bake at 350° for 20 minutes. Cut in bars while warm.

—*Mrs. Ivan Yoder, Ashland, OH*

Blueberry Snacking Bars

2 c. whole wheat flour
1 c. milk
½ c. honey
⅔ c. oil or butter
2½ tsp. baking powder
2 tsp. cinnamon

2 tsp. vanilla
¾ tsp. salt
3 eggs
3 c. blueberries
1 c. nuts

Mix together all except blueberries and nuts. Fold into nuts and blueberries. Bake at 350° for 45 minutes or until done. Cut into bars.

—*Ada Miller, Hazleton, IA*

An ounce of prevention is worth a pound of cure.

Saucy Bars

1 tsp. vanilla	1 tsp. soda
½ c. butter	½ tsp. salt
1 c. applesauce	½ tsp. cloves
1 egg	1 tsp. cinnamon
½ Tbsp. honey	1 tsp. nutmeg
2 c. whole grain flour	1 c. nuts, chopped
1 tsp. stevia	1 c. raisins

Cream vanilla, butter, applesauce, egg, and honey until fluffy. In a separate bowl, mix the rest of ingredients thoroughly. Add to applesauce-butter mixture and mix well. Put in 12" x 8" pan and bake 35 minutes at 350°.

—*Mrs. John Houston, Cottage Grove, TN*

Fudge Nut Bars

1 c. butter	**Filling:**
1⅓ c. sorghum	¾ c. carob powder
2½ c. whole wheat flour	2 tsp. cinnamon
1 tsp. soda	2 tsp. vanilla
3 c. rolled oats	½-⅔ c. sorghum or maple
2 eggs	syrup
2 tsp. vanilla	1 c. nuts, chopped
1 tsp. salt	¾ c. milk
	½ tsp. salt
	3 Tbsp. butter

Cream together butter and sorghum. Beat in eggs and vanilla. Sift and add flour, soda, and salt. Stir in oats. Set aside while you prepare filling. For filling, blend all ingredients together over low heat. Stir constantly, just until mixture comes to a slight boil. Spread two-thirds of oatmeal mixture evenly in a large jelly roll pan. Cover with filling. Dot with remaining dough and swirl it over filling. Bake at 350° for 25-30 minutes or until lightly browned.

—*Erma Hoover, Penn Yan, NY*

Date Bars

1⅓ c. whole wheat flour	1 c. honey
1 tsp. baking powder	1 tsp. pure vanilla extract
½ tsp. salt	1¾ c. dates, chopped
3 eggs	1 c. nuts, chopped

Mix flour with baking powder and salt. Beat eggs until very frothy in large mixing bowl. Gradually beat in honey, adding it in a fine stream. Add vanilla. Stir in flour, dates, and nuts. Mix well. Spread in a greased 9" x 13" x 2" pan. Bake at 350° for 35-45 minutes. Cool thoroughly. Cut into bars. Store tightly covered or freeze. Yield: about 3 dozen.

—*Mary E. Showalter, Mt. Solon, VA*

Sesame Seed Bars

⅔ c. honey	½ tsp. salt
¼ c. peanut butter (almond butter works too)	2½ c. sesame seeds
1 tsp. vanilla	1½ c. coconut

In a bowl, mix together first four ingredients. Add sesame seeds and coconut. Mix well. Press into 9" x 13" oiled baking dish with hands dipped in water. Bake at 300° for 30-40 minutes.

—*Loveda Bear, Patriot, OH*

Don't bite off more than you can chew.
Don't eat more than you can digest.

Oatmeal Fruit-Nut Bars

¾ c. rolled oats
¾ c. nuts, finely chopped
¼ c. wheat germ
1 tsp. ground cinnamon
⅓ c. apple juice concentrate
¾ c. pitted dates

¾ c. raisins
6 Tbsp. orange juice
  concentrate
2 tsp. grated orange zest,
  optional

Preheat oven to 350°. Process the oats in a blender or food processor to the consistency of coarse meal. Mix the oats, nuts, wheat germ, and cinnamon in a large bowl. Stir in the apple juice concentrate until mixture is crumbly. Reserve ½ c. of the oat mixture; press the remaining mixture into a nonstick 8" square baking pan. Process the dates, raisins, orange juice concentrate, and orange zest in the blender or food processor until the food is chopped, not pureed. Spread the fruit mixture evenly over the oat layer. Top with the reserved oat mixture and press it down firmly. Bake until lightly browned, 25-30 minutes. Cool completely; cut into squares or bars. Yield: about 30 bars.

—Katie Kuepfer, Milverton, Ontario

Delicious Bars

2 c. honey
½ c. butter, softened
2 c. whole wheat flour
2 eggs, beaten
1 c. carob chips or raisins
½ c. nuts, optional

1½ tsp. soda
1 tsp. baking powder
2 tsp. salt
2 tsp. vanilla
1 c. milk

Mix honey with butter and flour. Use a pastry blender or a fork. Save 1 c. of this crumb mixture for topping. To the remaining add the rest of the ingredients except chips/raisins and nuts. Pour into a greased 13" x 9" pan. Sprinkle with chips/raisins and nuts; cover with reserved crumbs. Bake at 350° for 25-30 minutes.

—Mrs. Vernon Hershberger, Loganville, WI

181

To ward off gnats and mosquitoes: Mix 1 Tbsp. vanilla in 1 c. water. Rub on skin. Safe for children and babies.

Remove rust streaks and food residue inside your refrigerator with a paste of baking soda and water. Most stains will vanish.

Unclog burners on a gas stove by boiling them in a strong baking powder solution. Such as ¼ box to 2 qt. water.

Soak material in buttermilk to remove mildew.

Stain remover: 3 Tbsp. borax and 1 Tbsp. lemon juice. Make a paste and rub in. Add 1 or 2 drops ammonia if spots persist.

Glue for china dishes: An excellent cement for mending broken china, etc. can be made by mixing flour with the white of an egg to a consistency of paste. Hot water does not injure it, but rather hardens this simple glue.

How to shell popcorn: Take a gunnysack, plastic or burlap, and put 6-8 ears of popcorn into it. Swing and hit bag on cement floor 3-4 times and most of your popcorn is shelled. There may be a little to shell off the ends. Dump out and repeat with more popcorn. Really saves your thumbs and time.

When using sun-dried sea salt use only half of the amount called for in a recipe. Dissolve in liquid before adding.

Yogurt can be used instead of sour cream in recipes asking for sour cream.

When converting a recipe asking for shortening or margarine use ¾ butter and ¼ oil. Example: 1 c. shortening = ¾ c. butter and ¼ c. oil.

Pies

Apple Pie

1½ c. cider, divided
1½ c. maple syrup
½ tsp. salt
1 c. raisins
3 Tbsp. (heaping) clear jel

3 eggs, separated
1 tsp. cinnamon
1 tsp. nutmeg
9 c. apples, peeled and
  shredded

Heat 1 c. cider, maple syrup, salt, and raisins. Mix clear jel, egg yolks, ½ c. cider, cinnamon, and nutmeg together. Add to first mixture. Boil until thick, then cool. Mix into peeled, shredded apples. Add beaten egg whites last. Pour into double crust and bake at 350° for 40 minutes or until pie filling bubbles.

—*Mrs. Joe Garber, Prattsburgh, NY*

Pumpkin Pie

1 c. pumpkin
1 egg, separated
1 Tbsp. whole wheat flour
1 tsp. pumpkin pie spice

½ tsp. salt
⅛ tsp. stevia (white extract)
2 c. milk

Heat the milk to almost boiling. Mix all ingredients except egg white. Beat egg white stiffly and add last. Stevia gives it a little different flavor. Pour into one unbaked pie shell. Bake at 400° for 10 minutes. Reduce heat to 350° and bake until set.

—*Malinda Yoder, Marion, KY*

*Housework is something you do that nobody
notices until you stop doing it.*

Fall Favorite Pumpkin Pie

1½ c. squash, pumpkin, or
    sweet potato, mashed
¾ c. honey, maple syrup, or
    grape concentrate
2 egg yolks, slightly beaten
½ tsp. salt
½ tsp. cinnamon
½ tsp. ginger
1 tsp. vanilla
1 tsp. butter
1½ c. rich milk, scalded

Mix all together, then add 2 egg whites, stiffly beaten, and fold into mixture. Pour into an unbaked pie shell and sprinkle with nutmeg. Bake at 375°-400° for 35-40 minutes or until custard sets.

—*Mrs. Junior Detweiler, Redding, IA*

Impossible Squash Pie

¼ c. honey
½ c. homemade Bisquick®
¾ c. milk
2 eggs
1 c. cooked squash
2½ tsp. pumpkin pie spice
2 tsp. vanilla

Heat oven to 350°. Grease a 9" or 10" pie pan. Beat all ingredients and pour into pan. Sprinkle with cinnamon. Bake 50-55 minutes or until knife inserted in center comes out clean.

—*Wilma Schmucker, Mio, MI*

Peach Cream Pie

1 c. light, sweet cream
2 Tbsp. flour
1 tsp. butter
1 unbaked pie shell
peaches, fresh sliced
¼ c. sucanat

Fill unbaked pie shell with thinly sliced peaches. Sprinkle sucanot over peaches. Mix cream, flour, and butter and pour over peaches. Bake without top crust in 350° oven for 40 minutes.

—*Mrs. Jesse Schlabach, Goshen, IN*

Maple Syrup Rhubarb Pie

1 egg, beaten	1 c. flour
½ c. flour	½ c. sucanat
1 c. maple syrup	¼ c. butter
2 c. rhubarb, chopped	

Beat egg and add flour, maple syrup, and rhubarb. Pour into unbaked pie shell. Mix together flour, sucanot, and butter. Spread over rhubarb. Bake at 350° for 45 minutes.

—*Elizabeth Drudge, Wroxeter, Ontario*

Old-Fashioned Cream Pie

⅓ c. flour	½ c. butter, melted
2 c. whipping cream,	½ c. maple syrup
unwhipped	1 unbaked 9" pie shell

Blend flour into melted butter. Add syrup; mix thoroughly. Add cream and stir until well blended. Pour into unbaked pie shell. Bake at 375° for 45-50 minutes. Cool before serving.

—*Mrs. Raymond Yutzy, Howe, IN*

Maple Nut Pie

Heat ½ c. milk and 1 c. maple syrup. Add 2 slightly beaten egg yolks and bring to a boil. Take off heat and add 1 Tbsp. gelatin soaked in ¼ c. water and chill until it starts to thicken a little. Fold in 2 stiffly beaten egg whites, 1 c. whipped cream, and ½ c. nut meats. Pour into baked pie crust and chill to set before serving.

—*Mrs. Edward J. Weaver, Ashland, OH*

Pecan Pie

3 eggs	1 tsp. vanilla
¾ c. maple syrup	1 c. pecans
2 Tbsp. butter, melted	1 unbaked 8" pie shell

Beat eggs, add syrup, and beat again. Stir in butter, vanilla, and pecans. Pour into unbaked pie shell. Bake at 350° for 35-45 minutes or until browned and center is just a little jiggly.

—Mrs. Raymond Yutzy, Howe, IN

Peanut Butter Pie

3¾ c. milk, divided	1 tsp. vanilla
⅓ c. honey	3 c. granola
⅛ tsp. salt	½ c. peanut butter
½ c. whole wheat flour	bananas
1 egg, separated	

Put 3 c. milk, honey, and salt in a kettle and bring to boiling. Beat flour, egg yolk, and ¾ c. milk together and add to boiling milk and cook for 1 minute. Remove from heat. Beat egg white and add a bit of pudding. Mix and add to rest of pudding. Add vanilla. When cold, mix granola and peanut butter and press ¾ of mixture into a pie pan. Add banana slices, if desired. Add pudding, rest of crumbs, and top with bananas.

—Mrs. Reuben Troyer, Rich Hill, MO

Blackberry Custard Pie

1 c. flour	⅛ tsp. salt
3 eggs, separated	½ tsp. cinnamon
3 c. milk	1 qt. blackberries or
1 c. honey	other fruit

Mix all ingredients together. Fold in beaten egg whites last. Pour into pie shells. Sprinkle with cinnamon. Bake at 375°. Remove from oven while custard is still soft and jiggly in center. Yield: 2 pies.

—Erma Hoover, Penn Yan, NY

Banana Cream Pie

1 c. white grape concentrate	6 egg yolks
or sweetener	6 c. milk
9 Tbsp. cornstarch	3 Tbsp. butter
¾ tsp. salt	1 Tbsp. vanilla

Heat milk. Mix first 4 ingredients and add to milk. Cook, stirring constantly, until thickened. Remove from heat and add butter and vanilla. Cool. Layer a pie shell with sliced bananas, pudding, and whipped cream. Can also be used for a pudding.

Variation: For chocolate pudding, add ½ c. carob powder to the cornstarch mixture.

—Mrs. Junior Detweiler, Redding, IA

Rhubarb Blueberry Pie

2½ c. rhubarb	Topping:
2 c. blueberries	5 Tbsp. butter
1 c. apple juice, divided	½ c. rolled oats
⅛ tsp. salt	¼ c. oat bran
1 tsp. cinnamon	½ c. whole grain flour
4 Tbsp. butter	¼ c. nuts

Combine fruit, ¼ c. apple juice, salt, and cinnamon and cook till boiling. Mix butter in ¾ c. apple juice. Add to fruit mixture. Stir while boiling for 2 minutes. Put in unbaked pie shell. Cover with topping. Bake at 375° for 10 minutes. Lower heat to 350° and bake for 35 more minutes.

—Emma Hoover, Bluff Point, NY

It's nice to be important, but more important to be nice.

Wheat Germ Pie Crust

1 c. wheat germ	4 Tbsp. butter
1 Tbsp. honey	½ tsp. cinnamon

Combine and press into 9" pie pan. Bake at 325° for 5-8 minutes. Cool and fill when ready to use.

—Mrs. J. T., Hestand, KY

Whole Wheat Pastry

3 c. whole wheat pastry flour	1 egg, slightly beaten
½ tsp. salt	1 Tbsp. vinegar
1 c. butter	5 Tbsp. cold water

Combine flour, salt, and butter. Blend together until crumbly. Combine egg, water, and vinegar. Stir into flour with fork until ingredients are moistened. With hands mold into a ball. Chill at least 15 minutes before rolling. Divide pastry in half and press into a ball. Roll out between 2 squares of waxed paper. Remove top sheet of paper and invert pastry over a pie pan, easing the pastry gently into the pan. Remove waxed paper and fit pastry into the pan without stretching. Roll out second half of pastry and place over filling, first having moistened edge of bottom pastry along rim of pan with water or milk to help secure bond. Press top and bottom pastries together along rim; trim off along edge and flute. Moisten top with back of a spoon dipped in milk to aid browning. Make a few vents in top to allow steam to escape. Bake according to directions. Makes enough pastry for a 2-crust 9" pie or 2 single crust pies. For pie shells, fit pastry into 2 pans, flute, and prick entire surface with fork. Bake at 450° for 8-10 minutes or until lightly browned.

—Mrs. Urie R. Miller, Shipshewana, IN

Pie Crust

1 c. spelt flour
⅛ tsp. stevia

½ tsp. baking powder
yogurt

Combine flour, stevia, baking powder, and enough yogurt to moisten. Knead until smooth. Roll out on well floured pastry cloth or cutting board. Gently peel crust from board and slide into greased and floured pie pan. Trim edges, fill, and bake. Crust will be crunchy and dense.

For a top crust: Cut 2 Tbsp. butter into 1 c. finely rolled oats. Add 1 tsp. cinnamon and a dusting of stevia and mix together. Spoon this topping over open fruit pie before baking.

Oatmeal Pie Crust

1 c. spelt four
⅔ c. rolled oats

¼ tsp. salt
⅓ c. oil

Combine dry ingredients. Gradually add oil. Pat dough into 9" pie pan. Bake at 400° for 10 minutes.

—*Laura Yoder, Free Union, VA*

The secret of success and happiness lies not in doing what you like, but in liking what you do.

Desserts
& Ice Cream

Quick Dessert

6 c. fruit	2 c. oats
⅔ c. whole wheat flour	⅓ c. butter, melted

Pour fruit into a glass cake pan. Mix flour, oats, and melted butter and put on top of fruit. Bake at 375° for 30 minutes.

—*Laura Yoder, Free Union, VA*

Cherry Pudding

1 c. sifted whole wheat flour	Sauce:
1 tsp. baking powder	1 c. pitted sour cherries,
⅛ tsp. salt	sweetened to taste
1 Tbsp. butter, melted	½ c. hot cherry juice
½ c. + 1 Tbsp. milk	1 Tbsp. butter, melted
¼-⅓ c. honey, sorghum, or maple syrup	

Sift together flour, baking powder, and salt. Add butter, milk, and sweetener; mix until blended. Pour into small baking pan. Cover with cherry sauce. Bake at 375° for 35-40 minutes or until done. Eat warm with milk or ice cream.

—*Mrs. Urie R. Miller, Shipshewana, IN*

When using honey as a sweetener in pudding, it is very important that you mix it to the milk before you add the cornstarch mixture, or the pudding will get thin.

Fruit Cobbler

½ c. honey
¼ c. butter
1 egg
½ c. milk
1 c. flour
2 tsp. baking powder
dash of salt

1 tsp. vanilla
2 c. fresh fruit, sliced
1 Tbsp. butter
⅓ c. honey
1 tsp. cinnamon
1 c. boiling water

Mix honey and butter. Add egg and beat well. Stir in milk. Stir in dry ingredients, then stir in vanilla. Spread evenly over bottom of 8" square baking pan. Mix remaining ingredients and pour over top of batter. Bake at 325° for 1-1¼ hours. Cake will rise to top during baking.

Note: We also use drained, canned fruit instead of fresh.

—*Mary Showalter, Mt. Solon, VA*

Blackberry Cobbler

Cobbler:
1½ c. whole wheat flour
¼ tsp. salt
2¼ tsp. baking powder
½ c. butter
⅓ c. milk
2 c. blackberries, fresh or frozen
½-1 tsp. cinnamon

Syrup:
1 c. maple syrup
1 c. water

½ c. butter

Mix flour, salt, and baking powder. Cut in butter till particles are like crumbs. Add milk and stir with a fork until dough leaves side of bowl. Roll out dough and spread with berries; sprinkle with cinnamon and roll up like jelly roll, and cut into 12 pieces. Melt ½ c. butter in 9" x 13" pan and arrange 12 pieces in 4 rows of 3 in pan. Mix syrup ingredients and pour over cobbler. Bake at 350° for 1 hour. Serve warm or cold.

—*Jolene Bontrager, Hillsboro, WI*

Maple Syrup Pudding

7 c. milk, divided
1 c. cornstarch
2 c. maple syrup

½ tsp. salt
8 egg yolks
4 Tbsp. butter

Bring 6 c. milk to a boil. Mix together remaining cup milk with cornstarch, maple syrup, and salt. Add to boiling milk. Take out 1 c. and mix with beaten egg yolks. Return to hot milk mixture. Stir until thickened on low heat. Add butter and stir to mix.

—*Mary Nolt, Withee, WI*

Jelled Carob Pudding

2 Tbsp. carob powder
2 Tbsp. honey
1 Tbsp. unflavored gelatin

3 Tbsp. water
2 c. milk

In a bowl, stir together carob, honey, gelatin, and cold water to a smooth paste. Heat milk to just below boiling and pour over carob paste, stirring. Simmer 2 minutes, stirring. Pour into a glass dish and refrigerate until completely set. If desired, garnish with whipped cream and carob curls.

Note: This is a simple but wholesome pudding which seems to agree well with troubled tummies.

—*Charlene Kennell, South Wayne, WI*

Skinny cooks can't be trusted.

Cornstarch Pudding

3 qt. milk, divided
1 c. cornstarch
½ c. finely ground flour
½ c. honey

1 tsp. salt
4 eggs, beaten
1 Tbsp. vanilla

Heat 2 qt. milk. Mix all the rest of the ingredients. Stir into hot milk with a wire whip. Continue to stir until mixture begins to thicken and boil. This is a good dessert, hot or cold. May be served with thickened fruit or mixed with yogurt.

—*Mrs. Mervin H. Yoder, Pleasant Hill, IL*

Steamed Pudding

2 c. whole wheat flour
1 tsp. soda
¼ tsp. salt
1 c. sorghum

1 c. sweet milk
1 c. raisins
1 tsp. cinnamon (or
    preferred spice)

Mix together flour, soda, and salt. In another bowl, mix the sorghum and milk, then mix with dry ingredients. Add raisins and cinnamon. Mix in casserole dish with a lid. Then set covered casserole dish in a larger cooker with sufficient water. Steam 3 hours.

—*Mary E. Showalter, Mt. Solon, VA*

Money saved at others' expense is greed.
Money saved at your own expense is frugality.

Date Pudding

1 c. boiling water	½ tsp. salt
1 c. dates, cut up	¼-⅓ c. maple syrup or sorghum
1½ c. whole wheat flour	1 egg
1 tsp. soda	2 Tbsp. butter, melted
1 tsp. baking powder	1 c. nuts

Pour boiling water over cut-up dates. Set aside to cool. Measure flour, soda, baking powder, and salt and sift into a bowl. Add maple syrup, egg, melted butter, date mixture, and nuts. Mix and pour into 13" x 9" baking pan. Pour sauce over top made up of the following:

1½ c. boiling water	2 Tbsp. butter
½ c. maple syrup	

Bake at 350° for 30 minutes or until done. Serve with whipped cream.

—*Mrs. Urie R. Miller, Shipshewana, IN*

Apple Rice Pudding

¼-⅓ c. maple syrup	2 c. cooked brown rice
2 Tbsp. butter	2 c. milk
¼ tsp. cinnamon	⅔ c. raisins
⅛ tsp. nutmeg	⅓ c. coconut, wheat germ, or
2 apples, chopped	sunflower seeds, optional

In a medium saucepan, heat maple syrup, butter, cinnamon, nutmeg, and apples until hot and bubbly. Add the cooked rice, milk, and raisins. Heat until mixture begins to bubble, but has not reached a full boil. Reduce the heat and simmer, stirring occasionally, until pudding thickens, about 15 minutes. Sprinkle with topping (coconut, etc.) and serve. This is also delicious without the toppings.

—*Malinda Yoder, Marion, KY*

Rice Pudding (Bengali Keer)

6 c. milk	¼ tsp. cardamom powder
¾ c. rice	½ bay leaf
½ c. raisins	½ c. honey

In large saucepan, combine milk, rice, and bay leaf. Cook on high heat for 15 minutes, stirring very frequently. Bring to a rolling boil and then lower heat. Simmer for 40 minutes or until thick. Remove bay leaf and add honey, raisins, and cardamom. Refrigerate until cold. Keer thickens as it cools. Serve cool.

—*Melissa Lapp, Cassadaga, NY*

Maple Tapioca

2 eggs	¼ tsp. salt
1 c. maple syrup	½ c. tapioca
4 c. milk	

Beat eggs and add rest of ingredients in heavy saucepan. Cook until thick, stirring almost constantly.

—*Elizabeth Drudge, Wroxeter, Ontario*

Tapioca Jello

2 qt. water	¾ c. honey (1½ c. for
2 c. tapioca	strawberry)
2 c. papaya, peach, or	3 Tbsp. unflavored gelatin
strawberry concentrate	6 c. water

Bring 2 qt. water and tapioca to a boil. Cook until tapioca is clear, stirring every once in a while. In the meantime, dissolve gelatin in 1 of the 6 c. water. Bring 2 c. water to boil and add honey and gelatin. Add fruit concentrate and remainder of water. Mix with tapioca. Yield: 1 gal.

—*Loveda Bear, Patriot, OH*

Rhubarb Tapioca

1 qt. strawberries
1 c. pearl tapioca
2 c. hot water
2 c. rhubarb
2 c. fruit juice or cold water

1 c. maple syrup
⅛ tsp. salt
½ tsp. cinnamon
1 tsp. vanilla, optional

Soak tapioca for several hours or overnight. If canned strawberries are used you can use 2 c. of the juice instead of the water to soak the tapioca in, otherwise you can use water. Add remaining ingredients (except strawberries, cinnamon, and vanilla) and cook, stirring often, until tapioca is clear or nearly clear. Add strawberries, cinnamon, and vanilla.

—Mrs. Joe Garber, Prattsburgh, NY

Nutritional Autumn Salad

4 c. apples, chopped
1 c. carrots, shredded
½ c. raisins

½ c. sunflower seeds
bananas, optional

Mix together and enjoy this simple but nutritious dish as your fruit.
—Mrs. Ervin Bontrager, Hillsboro, WI

Frozen Fruit

4 c. water
1 c. maple syrup
¾ c. clear jel

½ c. tapioca, optional
1 pkg. frozen fruit

Cook all ingredients together, except the fruit, until thick. Add fruit. Strawberries, cherries, raspberries, apricots, or peaches are all delicious this way. Amounts of water, maple syrup, and clear jel can be varied depending on how thick you like your fruit or how big your package of frozen fruit is.

—Elizabeth Drudge, Wroxeter, Ontario

Healthful Jello

2 Tbsp. unflavored gelatin   1 c. boiling water
a tiny pinch of stevia extract   1 c. cold water
1 Tbsp. fruit juice

Dissolve gelatin, stevia, and fruit juice in hot water. Then add cold water. Refrigerate until set.

—*Mrs. Simon Borntrager, Beeville, TX*

Aunt Betty's Cider Blocks

Heat 6 c. cider. Sprinkle 6 Tbsp. unflavored gelatin over 2 c. cold cider. Dump together and stir to dissolve soaked gelatin in hot cider. Pour into flat pan and cool till set. Can use any juice except pineapple.

—*Laura Royer, Camden, IN*

Citrus Gelatin Blocks

4 Tbsp. plain gelatin   ⅓ c. honey or desired
1 c. cold water   sweetener to taste
2 c. boiling water   2 Tbsp. lemon juice
1 c. undiluted orange juice concentrate

Stir gelatin and cold water together. Allow to set 1 minute. Add boiling water, stirring until dissolved. Add remaining ingredients. Stir well and chill in a 9" x 13" pan until set. Cut into small squares and serve chilled.

—*Charlene Kennell, South Wayne, WI*

Fruit Gelatin

1 Tbsp. unflavored gelatin
2 Tbsp. cold water
¼ c. honey

1 c. boiling water
1 c. mixed fruit, diced

Soak gelatin in cold water 5 minutes. Add boiling water and honey. Stir until dissolved. Cool. Drain fruit and stir lightly into gelatin when congealing starts. Turn into molds or pans. Chill. Cut and serve.

—*Laura Royer, Camden, IN*

Strawberry Rhubarb Stew

4 c. water
4 c. rhubarb, ½" slices
4 c. strawberries, sliced
1 c. honey

¼ c. whole wheat flour
¾ tsp. cinnamon
½ tsp. sea salt

Put all ingredients in a pot and stir. Bring to a boil. Reduce heat and simmer until rhubarb is tender or for 10-15 minutes.

—*Mrs. John J. Miller, Millersburg, OH*

Edith's Vanilla Custard

14 eggs
¾ c. honey
5 c. milk

1 tsp. vanilla
1 tsp. cinnamon
½ tsp. nutmeg, optional

Mix all together until fully blended. Pour into an 8" x 13" glass baking dish. Lightly sprinkle top with nutmeg. Place in preheated 350° oven for 1 hour or until knife inserted comes out clean. Remove from oven when custard has fully set. After fully chilled, cut and serve as 3" x 3" squares. Keep refrigerated.

—*Laura Royer, Camden, IN*

Sweet Potato Custard

1 qt. milk, scalded
½ c. honey
¼ tsp. salt
1 tsp. cinnamon

6 eggs, beaten
1 c. sweet potatoes or squash
1 Tbsp. vanilla

Blend everything together in a blender. Pour into a 1½-qt. baking dish. Set into a pan of water. Bake at 400°-450° for an hour until set or until a knife stuck in the center comes out clean.

—*Pauline Schrock, Clayton, IL*

Baked Custard

¾ c. honey or grape
  concentrate
1 qt. milk, scalded

nutmeg for garnishing
6 eggs, separated
⅛ tsp. salt

Beat egg yolks; add rest of ingredients then beaten egg whites. Pour into baking pan then set into a pan of hot water. Bake at 350° or until knife inserted in center comes out clean.

Variations: Sprinkle ½ c. unsweetened coconut over custard just before baking. Or add 1 Tbsp. carob powder to egg yolks. Or add 1 c. cooked pumpkin, squash, or sweet potatoes. Or add ½ c. cooked rice.

—*Mrs. Junior Detweiler, Redding, IA*

Modern manufacturing of sugar has brought about entirely new diseases. The sugar of commerce is nothing else but concentrated crystallized acid.
—*Dr. Robert Boesler, 1912*

Pumpkin Chiffon Custard

1 c. honey	2 c. milk
2 Tbsp. unflavored gelatin	2 c. cooked pumpkin, mashed
2 tsp. cinnamon	1 c. cream
1 tsp. nutmeg	1¼ c. toasted coconut
½ tsp. salt	butter
6 eggs, separated	

Mix together first 5 ingredients. Set aside. Beat egg yolks and add milk. Mix with first mixture and heat, bringing it to a boil. Take off heat and stir in mashed pumpkin. Chill until partly set. In separate bowls, beat the egg whites and cream; add to chilled mixture. Makes 2 qt. custard. Rub sides of bowl with butter and line with toasted coconut. Dip custard into coconut-lined bowl.

—*Mary E. Showalter, Mt. Solon, VA*

Aunt Eva's Caramel Apples

8 c. apples, sliced	1¾-2 c. milk
¾ c. honey	2 Tbsp. (heaping) cornstarch
¼ c. sorghum	vanilla or butter, optional
¾ c. water	

Mix apples, honey, sorghum, and water and put in saucepan on stove until cooked. Mix the milk and cornstarch together, then mix into the cooked mixture while still on the stove. It will look curdly for a while then turn smooth. Take off heat and cool. It will get more thick as it cools.

—*Laura Royer, Camden, IN*

It isn't necessary to blow out the other
fellow's light to let yours shine.

Rhubarb Crunch

1 c. whole wheat flour
1 c. rolled oats
½ c. sucanat
½ c. butter, melted

4 c. rhubarb, diced
1½ c. water
1½ c. maple syrup

Mix together flour, oats, sucanot, and butter. Press half of this mixture into a 9" x 13" baking dish. Spread with rhubarb. Mix together water and syrup and pour over rhubarb. Top with remaining crumbs. Bake at 350° for 1 hour or until done.

—Elizabeth Drudge, Wroxeter, Ontario

Rhubarb Crisp

4 c. rhubarb
½ c. honey
½ c. whole wheat flour
½ tsp. cinnamon
1 Tbsp. water

Crumbs:
1 c. whole wheat flour
½ c. oatmeal
¾ c. honey
½ c. butter, melted

Combine first 5 ingredients. Press into a greased 8" x 8" pan. Set aside. Combine crumb ingredients. Mix well. Sprinkle over rhubarb mixture. Bake uncovered at 375° for 35 minutes or until golden brown.

—Mrs. John J. Miller, Millersburg, OH

The Bible promises no loaves for the loafer.

Apple Dumplings

2 c. whole wheat flour
2½ tsp. baking powder
½ tsp. salt
⅔ c. butter or olive oil
½ c. milk
6 apples, peeled, cored, and quartered

Syrup:
2 c. maple syrup
2 c. water

Make a pastry by mixing all ingredients except apples. Roll out and cut into squares. Place a quarter of an apple on each pastry square and fold up and place in baking dish. Mix syrup ingredients and pour over apples. Bake at 350° for 45 minutes. Serve warm.

—*Elizabeth Drudge, Wroxeter, Ontario*

Apple Crunch

4-5 c. apples, peeled and
  chopped
1 c. raisins
2 tsp. cinnamon
⅛ tsp. salt
½ c. water

1 c. oatmeal
1½ c. whole wheat flour
⅛ tsp. salt
½ c. honey
⅔ c. soft butter

Mix apples, raisins, cinnamon, salt, and water and place in baking dish. Mix rest of ingredients and arrange on top of apples. Bake 30 minutes at 350° or until golden brown. Serve hot with ice cream or cold milk.

—*Mrs. Junior Detweiler, Redding, IA*

The race isn't always to the swift, but to
the ones that keep on running.

Apple Crisp

6-7 c. apples, sliced	2 c. oatmeal
1¼ c. honey, divided	½ tsp. allspice
1 tsp. cinnamon	¼ tsp. nutmeg
2 c. whole wheat pastry flour	½ c. chicken fat

Mix together apples, ½ c. honey, and cinnamon. Place in cake pan. Mix together flour, oatmeal, allspice, and nutmeg. Blend the remaining ¾ c. of honey with the chicken fat and mix with flour mixture until crumbly. Put crumbs on top of apples. Bake at 350° until apples are tender or soft.

—Laura Royer, Camden, IN

Cherry Dumplings

4 c. cherries	⅛ c. sweetener (maple
½ c. maple syrup	syrup or honey)
3 c. water	¼ c. milk
1½ c. whole wheat flour	1 egg
2 tsp. baking powder	½ tsp. salt

In a large kettle, bring cherries, maple syrup, and water to a boil. In a bowl, mix together rest of ingredients. Drop by spoonsful in boiling juice. Cover and simmer 12 minutes.

—Mary Nolt, Withee, WI

Ginger Dumplings

1 Tbsp. butter	⅛ tsp. salt
1 Tbsp. honey	½ tsp. ginger
¼ c. sorghum	1 tsp. baking powder
¼ c. sweet milk	1 c. or more whole wheat flour
½ tsp. soda	canned peaches or pears

Mix first 6 ingredients together well. Add ginger, baking powder, and flour. Mix to a stiff dough. Heat fruit to boiling and drop stiff dough by spoonsful into boiling fruit. Simmer, tightly covered, for 15 minutes. Serve with milk. Can be made with berries also.

—Mary E. Showalter, Mt. Solon, VA

Pineapple Rings

8 slices pineapple
¾ c. natural peanut butter
¼ c. plain yogurt
¼ c. maple syrup

¾ c. whipping cream
2 Tbsp. maple syrup
⅛ tsp. cinnamon
⅛ tsp. salt

Mix together peanut butter, yogurt, and maple syrup until creamy. Spoon on top of pineapple rings. Whip the cream until desired stiffness; add maple syrup, salt, and cinnamon. Put on top of rings. Chill and serve.

Tip: For good peanut butter mix 16 oz. natural peanut butter with ¼ c. sorghum. Stir well to mix.

—Mrs. Raymond Yutzy, Howe, IN

Ice Cream Sandwiches

Crust:
½ c. quick oats
½ c. whole wheat flour
¼ tsp. soda
⅔ c. butter
1 Tbsp. carob, optional
2 Tbsp. honey

Filling:
2 c. cream
4 eggs, separated
½ c. maple syrup (or more
  if desired)
flavoring of your choice

Combine dry ingredients. Cut in butter until mixture is crumbly. Add honey. Pat or crumble into jelly roll pan and bake at 350° until crusty. Cool.

Filling: Beat egg whites, cream, and egg yolks in separate bowls. Fold a little cream into egg yolks first then fold all together. Fold in sweetener and flavoring of your choice. Pour onto crust and set out to freeze at 0° or under. Cover pan to keep out predators.

—Jolene Bontrager, Hillsboro, WI

Healthy Homemade Ice Cream

1 gal. whole milk, divided	¼ c. lemon juice
1 dozen eggs	3 Tbsp. Knox® gelatin
1 qt. maple syrup	1 qt. red raspberries or
1 tsp. vanilla	strawberries
1 tsp. almond flavoring	(preferably canned)

Soak gelatin in 1 c. milk. Heat until dissolved. Beat eggs in a large bowl, add milk, gelatin mixture, maple syrup, and flavorings. Last of all add fruit. This is enough to fill a 2-gal. freezer. It can also be made in smaller batches for smaller freezers.

Variation: Omit fruit and almond flavoring for vanilla ice cream.

—*Jolene Bontrager, Hillsboro, WI*

Banana-Nut Ice Cream

1 gal. milk	1 Tbsp. vanilla
1⅓ c. cornstarch	1 pt. maple syrup
8 eggs	1 c. chopped pecans,
1 pt. milk	roasted
1 tsp. salt	2-3 bananas, mashed

Heat 1 gal. milk to scalding. In the meantime, mix the pint milk, eggs, salt, and cornstarch and beat well. Pour into scalded milk. Stir often as it thickens. Boil several minutes, stirring constantly. Take off heat and pour through sieve. Add vanilla and maple syrup. Stir well and cool thoroughly. Enough for 1½-gal. freezer. When almost done freezing, add bananas and nuts, if desired. When adding bananas and nuts, don't use all the pudding as it makes the freezer too full. To roast nuts, mix ½ Tbsp. melted butter with 1 c. chopped nuts. Spread onto cookie sheet and put in 275° oven for 1 hour, stirring every 10-15 minutes.

—*Mrs. Raymond Yutzy, Howe, IN*

Pure Maple Syrup Ice Cream

2 c. pure maple syrup	1 Tbsp. vanilla
7 eggs	1 c. nuts, chopped
2½ qt. milk	2 c. whipping cream
¼ tsp. sea salt	

Beat maple syrup and eggs together. Add milk and salt. Cook over medium heat, stirring constantly, until milk coats a spoon or becomes slightly thickened. Cool for several hours. Add vanilla and nuts. Whip the cream and fold it into the custard mixture. Place in gallon freezer and freeze.

—Mary S. Yoder, Wooster, OH

Lemon Sherbet

1 c. whipping cream	juice from 1 lemon
1 c. plain yogurt	1½ tsp. lemon peel, grated
⅔ c. maple syrup	

In a bowl, combine cream and maple syrup. Whip until stiff. Fold in lemon juice, yogurt, and lemon peel. Leave in bowl and put in freezer. Stir every 45 minutes until frozen (about 5 hours).

—Melissa Lapp, Cassadaga, NY

Homemade Sherbet

1 Tbsp. unflavored gelatin	2 Tbsp. lemon juice
1 c. water	2 c. milk
9 oz. unsweetened frozen juice concentrate	honey to taste

Sprinkle gelatin over water. Stir in honey. Heat gently just until gelatin is dissolved. Add lemon juice and juice concentrate. Stir in milk. Freeze in a small ice cream freezer, according to manufacturer's instructions, or freeze in a pan in deep freeze until nearly frozen, stir or beat mixture, and return to freezer until solid. Allow to thaw slightly before serving.

Note: Any fruit juice concentrate desired may be used in this recipe. Raspberry is good.

—Charlene Kennell, South Wayne, WI

Crackers, Dips, & Snacks

Graham Crackers

½ c. olive oil
½ c. honey
1 Tbsp. molasses
2 tsp. vanilla
½ tsp. salt

3½ c. wheat flour
1½ tsp. baking powder
2 tsp. cinnamon
⅓ c. milk

Mix liquids first except milk, then add dry ingredients alternately with milk. If dough is too sticky add more flour. Divide into quarters then roll to ¼" thick with rolling pin. Cut in squares. Place on cookie sheets and prick with fork. Bake at 300° until edges are slightly brown. Cool a little on cookie sheets before removing. These freeze well in airtight container.

—*Mrs. Naomi Ruth Bontrager, Mio, MI*

Graham Crackers

1 c. honey
1 c. butter
½ c. sweet milk
2 eggs, beaten

6 c. whole wheat flour
2 tsp. soda
2½ tsp. baking powder
⅛ tsp. salt

Cream together honey and butter. Add milk and eggs. Add dry ingredients and stir well. Roll dough thin and cut. Place on cookie sheets and bake at 350°, turning once during baking time. Bake until crackers do not dent to a fingernail. They do crisp up a little after cooling. Watch carefully during last couple minutes as they can burn easily.

—*Joanna Frantz, Camden, IN*

To get to Heaven, turn right and go straight.

CRACKERS, DIPS, & SNACKS

Oatmeal Crackers

3 c. rolled oats
1 c. raw wheat germ
2 c. whole wheat flour
½ c. sesame seeds, optional

3 Tbsp. honey
¾ c. oil
1 c. water

Mix dry ingredients in a large bowl. Heat water, oil, and honey till quite warm. Pour over oat mixture. Mix well and roll out on floured board until ⅛" thick. Cut in squares. Put on cookie sheet and salt lightly. Bake at 300° for 20-25 minutes until crisp, but not too brown.

—*Melissa Lapp, Cassadaga, NY*

Crispy Cracker Wheels

5 c. spelt or wheat flour
1½ tsp. salt
1 Tbsp. yeast
1⅔ c. hot water

sesame seeds, poppy
seeds, coarse salt, chili
powder, etc. as desired

Place one oven rack as high as possible in oven, and the other near the middle. Preheat oven to 375°. Combine all ingredients. Knead several minutes until smooth on a lightly floured board. Divide into 12-18 balls (depending on size of cracker you desire). Allow to rest 10 minutes, covered. Roll each ball into a 6" round. (Larger or smaller, as preferred. Thinner circles make crispier crackers, thicker will make them crunchier and chewier.) Place 2 on a greased baking sheet. Prick with fork; sprinkle with salt and choice of spices or seeds. Bake on middle rack until the cracker will slide around on the sheet when shaken. Slide crackers off baking sheet onto the top rack. Continue baking until crisp and golden. Repeat until all the crackers are baked. Cool completely and store in an airtight container. Top with egg, chicken, or tuna salad if desired.

—*Charlene Kennell, South Wayne, WI*

Whole Wheat Crackers

7 c. whole wheat flour
1 c. butter
1 tsp. salt
1 tsp. baking powder

1 tsp. soda
1 tsp. cream of tartar
1½ c. milk or water

Mix as for pie dough. Roll thin and cut in squares. Prick with fork and place on cookie sheet. Bake at 375° until done (lightly browned).

—*Eva Troyer, Scottsville, KY*

Vegetable Dip

1 c. sour cream
1 Tbsp. parsley flakes
½ tsp. onion salt

1 c. Miracle Whip®
½ tsp. garlic salt

Mix all ingredients together. Chill and serve.

—*Erma Hoover, Penn Yan, NY*

Prairie Fire Pinto Dip

2 c. cooked pinto beans
1 c. cheese, shredded
½-¾ c. water
2-3 Tbsp. butter

2 Tbsp. minced onion
4 tsp. chili powder
dash of garlic powder

Combine all ingredients in a small saucepan. Cook over low heat until cheese melts. Serve hot with tortilla chips.

—*Charlene Kennell, South Wayne, WI*

Garbanzo Bean Spread

½ onion, chopped
2 Tbsp. olive oil
2 tsp. dried parsley
1 tsp. dried basil
½ tsp. dried oregano
dash of garlic salt
dash of cumin

juice of 1 lemon
salt to taste
3 c. cooked garbanzo beans,
   (may use canned)
   mashed, ground, or
   blended with as little
   water as possible

Sauté onion in oil until soft. Add herbs at the last minute. Mix all ingredients thoroughly, cover and chill. Serve as a spread on whole grain breads or served with "dippers" – tortilla chips, melbas, crackers, etc.

—*Charlene Kennell, South Wayne, WI*

Crispy, Crunchy Corn Chips

1 c. cornmeal
½ c. whole wheat pastry flour
½ tsp. soda

¼ tsp. salt
3 Tbsp. oil
⅓ c. milk

Mix together dry ingredients. Gradually stir in oil that has been mixed with milk. Knead 2 minutes on floured board. Roll out very thin on cookie sheet. Sprinkle lightly with cheese powder if desired. Bake at 350° for 8-10 minutes or until golden brown. Good in salads.

—*Mrs. Esther Yoder, Hillsboro, WI*

"Doc, am I getting better?"
"I don't know. Let me feel your purse."

213

Soft Pretzels

Using your favorite bread recipe, mix dough and let it rise as for bread. Shape the dough into pretzels. Mix ½ c. warm water with 4 tsp. soda. Dip pretzels into soda water and place on greased cookie sheets. Sprinkle with coarse salt. Let rise 15 minutes. Bake at 350° for 15 minutes. Brush with butter. Serve with honey mustard dip. (Equal parts of honey and mustard mixed together.)

—*Mrs. Raymond Yutzy, Howe, IN*

Wheat Germ Sticks

1 tsp. baking powder	¼ c. butter
¾ c. raw wheat germ	2 Tbsp. milk
⅛ tsp. salt	1 egg white
1 Tbsp. minced onion or chives	¼ c. raw wheat germ

Mix together baking powder, ¾ c. wheat germ, salt, and onion. Cut in butter. Stir in 1 Tbsp. of the milk and egg white. Shape in ball. Roll out with floured rolling pin on floured surface to about ⅛" thick. Cut into sticks. Brush with final Tbsp. milk and roll in wheat germ. Place on ungreased baking sheets. Bake for 6 minutes or until golden brown at 400°.

—*Iva Kauffman, Monroe, WI*

> *Wherefore whosoever shall eat this bread, and drink this cup of the Lord, unworthily, shall be guilty of the body and blood of the Lord. For this cause many are weak and sickly among you, and many sleep.*
> —*I Corinthians 11:27, 30*

Potato Chips

2 lb. (4 large) potatoes, peeled or unpeeled and very
   thinly sliced
4 c. oil   salt

As potatoes are sliced, immediately drop them into a bowl of very cold water. Heat oil in a heavy skillet to 360°. Meanwhile, drain potatoes very well (they should not be in the cold water very long). Lay slices in a single layer on a clean dishcloth and cover with another one. In batches, and maintaining oil temperature at 360°, fry slices for 4 minutes or until golden brown. With a slotted spoon, transfer chips to newspaper or brown paper bag to drain (chips drained on paper towels won't remain crisp). Sprinkle with salt and serve.

—Mrs. Raymond Yutzy, Howe, IN

More-ish Apples

4 apples   ¼ c. honey
¼ c. home-ground peanut butter

Mix honey and peanut butter. Spread in core (holes) in apple halves. Enjoy!

—Mary E. Beachy, Liberty, KY

Apple Delight

8 apples, cored and diced   ½-1 c. honey
2 c. organic raisins   2 Tbsp. cinnamon
1 lemon, juiced

Cover raisins with warm water and soak for 10 minutes. Drain, discard water, and mix all ingredients together. Chill and serve for lunch or a snack.

—Mrs. John J. Miller, Millersburg, OH

Eggplant Snack Stick

1 medium eggplant (1¼ lb.)	¾ tsp. garlic salt
½ c. toasted wheat germ	½ c. egg substitute
½ c. Parmesan cheese, grated	1 c. spaghetti sauce,
1 tsp. Italian seasoning	warmed

Cut eggplant lengthwise into ½" thick slices, then cut each slice lengthwise into ½" strips. In a shallow dish, combine the wheat germ, Parmesan cheese, Italian seasoning, and garlic salt. Dip eggplant sticks into eggs, then coat with wheat germ mixture. Arrange in a single layer on a greased baking dish. Sprinkle eggplant with melted butter or oil. Broil 4" from heat for 3 minutes. Remove from heat. Turn sticks and sprinkle again. Broil 2 minutes longer or until golden brown. Serve immediately with spaghetti sauce. Yield: 8 servings.

—*Mrs. Leroy B. Miller, Middlefield, OH*

Homemade Peanut Butter

2 lb. organic roasted peanuts	enough maple syrup to
¼ c. olive oil	suit your taste

Put everything in blender and blend till smooth. Refrigerate.

—*Mrs. John J. Miller, Millersburg, OH*

High-Fiber Balls

1 c. peanut butter	1 c. coconut
1 c. honey	½ c. bran
1 c. raisins	3 c. oatmeal
1 c. carob chips	¼ tsp. salt

Stir and make firm balls and freeze (optional).

—*Regina Rose Esh, age 7, Burkesville, KY*

Yum Yum Balls

½ c. natural peanut butter
2 c. unsweetened shredded
   coconut
¼ c. chopped cashews
1 Tbsp. orange juice

½ c. chopped dates
½ c. raw sunflower seeds
¼ c. honey
½ c. raisins

Combine all ingredients and mix well; roll into 1" balls and press like a patty. Place on ungreased cookie sheet and refrigerate until firm. Store in closed container in a cold place. Yield: 3 dozen.

—Mrs. Abe Bontrager, Dalton, WI

Fruit Balls

Equal parts of:
raisins
coconut

dates

Add as desired:
sunflower seeds
English walnuts
pecans

orange juice or other fruit
   juice
honey

Grind together and shape into balls.

—Laura Royer, Camden, IN

*See Jesus in everything, and in
everything you will find a blessing.*

Wholesome Pecans

Fill a wide-mouthed quart jar with pecans. Add 1 Tbsp. Real salt and fill with water. Let soak at room temperature for 8-10 hours. Drain; spread nuts on a stainless steel pan and dry in a warm oven, not over 150°. Stir occasionally and dry until nice and crisp. Store in airtight container.

Walnuts, peanuts, almonds, and cashews can also be used instead of pecans. Cashews, however, should be soaked not more than 5-6 hours and dried faster in a hotter oven (200°-250°). Nuts that have been soaked then dried are easier to digest and their nutrients are more readily available.

—Raymond Yutzy, Howe, IN

Homemade Trail Mix

7 c. oatmeal	2 c. honey
1 c. wheat germ	3 c. raisins
2 tsp. cinnamon	3 c. chopped dates or
½ c. butter, melted	dried fruit of your
1½ c. peanuts or almonds	choice
½ tsp. salt	

Mix oatmeal, wheat germ, salt, cinnamon, and nuts together. Melt butter and honey together. Pour over dry mixture and mix well. Spread on cookie sheet and bake for 25-30 minutes at 300°. Cool; break in pieces and add dried fruit of your choice.

—Thelma Zook, Oakland, MD

Opportunities are never lost.
Someone will take the ones you miss.

Cheese & Yogurt

Wholesome Cultured Foods

The culturing of dairy products such as yogurt and kefir makes it easier to digest by breaking down some of the lactose and casein. This also supplies our bodies with much-needed enzymes and beneficial bacteria.

Culturing or lacto-fermenting was a means of preserving and predigesting foods that people have used for ages. It was especially favored for the young or sick. This form of pro-biotics helps to provide protection against diseases by keeping intestinal bacteria in proper balance.

If you have a shortage of digestive enzymes it may cause a nutritional deficiency and food allergies. A congested liver and an overworked pancreas cannot always produce enough enzymes to properly digest foods. We may be eating healthy foods, but without sufficient enzymes and good bacteria the nutrients will just pass on through.

The discretion of a man deferreth his anger; and it is his glory

to pass over a trangession.

—Proverbs 19:11

Homemade Mozzarella Cheese

4 gal. whole milk   **1 tsp. rennet**
5 tsp. citric acid   **⅓ c. salt**

Stir citric acid into ½ c. cold water until dissolved. Stir into cool milk and mix 2 minutes. Heat to 88°. Add rennet in additional ½ c. cool water. Stir well. Allow to coagulate (approximately 30-60 minutes). Cut into ½" cubes with a long knife. Gently heat to 108°, stirring carefully. Drain into colander. Heat 3 qt. water with salt to 160°. Place cheese lump in water. Let set to soften slightly. Stretch cheese with 2 long forks. Pull cheese up and apart, much like pulling taffy. When cheese has a smooth consistency, about 5-10 minutes, remove from water and knead on a clean surface until "plastic". Place into a mold (a 1-qt. container works well) and place mold into a kettle of ice water. Once chilled, cheese is ready to slice and eat. Refrigerate. Freeze after one week.

—Charlene Kennell, South Wayne, WI

Cracker Barrel Cheddar Cheese

½ c. sesame tahini   **¼ c. Nutritional Yeast**
4 oz. pimentos   **Flakes**
3 Tbsp. Emes® unflavored   **1 tsp. salt**
** gelatin**   **1 tsp. onion powder**
½ c. cold water   **½ tsp. garlic powder**
¼ c. lemon juice   **½ c. boiling water**

Dissolve gelatin in cold water. Put all ingredients in blender or Vita-Mix, adding water last. Blend until creamy and pour into mold or you can use as a dip or other cheese dishes. Freezes well and shreds.

—Mrs. Joni Troyer, Millersburg, OH

Simple Cheese

Heat 2 gal. milk to 180°. Remove from heat and add ½ c. apple cider vinegar. Stir until it separates. Pour curds into a colander lined with a cheesecloth and set on a pail. Mix in 2½ tsp. salt with a fork. Place in a cheese press or a No. 10 can with both ends cut out, set in a colander. Fill a 2-qt. jar with water and set on top of curds for a weight. Curds must be hot so they will hang together.

Variations: Add dried, ground jalapeno peppers. Or for more flavorful cheese, use aged milk or buttermilk. Goats' milk may also be used.

—Amelia Troyer, Glenford, OH

Velveeta Cheese

2 gal. thick sour milk   1 c. cream or milk
1 tsp. soda   6 Tbsp. butter
2 tsp. salt

Scald sour milk to 115°. Put in strainer and let drain until completely dry. Transfer curds to bowl and rub soda into curds. Let set 2 hours. Melt butter in top of double boiler; add curds and heat till all is dissolved. Add cream gradually. Heat till desired consistency. Cover while cooling to avoid a skin on top. It will thicken as it cools.

—Susie Schlabach, Goshen, IN

Simple pleasures are easily found.

Mexican-Style Yogurt Cheese

2 c. plain yogurt
1 c. prepared salsa

2 Tbsp. fresh cilantro
leaves, chopped, optional

In a small bowl, combine yogurt and salsa. Mix well. Spoon the yogurt mixture into a strainer lined with muslin or a coffee filter. Place a bowl under the strainer to catch the liquid (whey) that drains from the yogurt. Cover and refrigerate 12 hours. Discard liquid. Add cilantro; mix well. Add salt and pepper to taste.

—*Laura Yoder, Free Union, VA*

Muenster Cheese

2½ gal. sour milk. Let set till thick like junket. Scald till it is too hot to hold your hand in, then pour into cheesecloth. Let hang until curds are dry – overnight or about 12 hours. Crumble curds and mix 2 heaping tsp. soda and ½ c. butter into them. Let set for 2 hours, then put in double boiler. Add 1 c. sour cream and melt. When melted, add another cup of sour cream and 1 Tbsp. salt. Mix well; pour into a buttered mold. Let set until completely cold and slice.

—*Mrs. John A. Mast, Dundee, OH*

Easy Cheese

1 gal. sweet milk
1¼ tsp. citric acid (dissolved
  in a little water)

¼ tablet cheese rennet
½ Tbsp. salt

Heat milk and citric acid to 88°. Remove from heat. Add rennet. Cover and let set 15 minutes. Cut into curds. Let set 10 minutes. Heat till curds hang together. Drain. Add salt. Press into square container and cool for slicing cheese or use as curds to eat fresh.

—*Mrs. Mervin H. Yoder, Pleasant Hill, IL*

Cottage Cheese

Heat 2 gal. fresh milk to barely lukewarm. Add ¼ tablet rennet dissolved in a little water. Let set until firm. Cut in small curds. Heat till very warm, 100°-106°, stirring so curds do not mat. Keep at this temperature 5 minutes. Drain quickly and rinse with cold water. Add salt to taste and a little fresh milk or cream.

—Mrs. Mervin Yoder, Pleasant Hill, IL

Cottage Cheese

Heat to boiling 1 gal. milk. Pour in ½ c. apple cider vinegar. Stir. It will curdle immediately. Let set until cooled. Pour through colander to drain. Add enough cream to right consistency and salt to taste.

—Mrs. Raymond Yutzy, Howe, IN

Sweet Cream Butter

Collect cream and keep refrigerated until you have enough to churn. Place in a saucepan and heat over medium heat until just below the boiling point. Allow to cool, then chill overnight. Remove cream from the refrigerator and let set until the temperature is 50°-60°. Churn. I use a blender and churn butter in batches. As soon as the cream changes into butter, pour into cheesecloth-lined strainer. Allow to drain undisturbed until all butter has been churned. Run cold water over butter particles until water runs clear. Work butter into ball, pressing out excess water. Salt to taste. Will remain sweet longer than unpasteurized butter.

—Charlene Kennell, South Wayne, WI

Yogurt

Heat 1 gal. milk to 190°. Take off heat and add 2¼ Tbsp. unflavored gelatin that has been soaked in ½ c. cold water. Stir well. Cool to 130°. Add 2 Tbsp. vanilla (optional), ¼ c. plain yogurt, and ½-¾ c. honey. Beat until smooth. Cover and put in oven with just the pilot on for 8 hours or overnight. Chill. For flavored yogurt, pie filling, preserves, or peanut butter can be added. For plain yogurt, omit flavoring.

—*Miriam Yoder, Baltic, OH*

Yogurt (Large Family Recipe)

Heat 2 gal. milk to 180°. Dissolve 5½ Tbsp. plain gelatin in 1¼ c. cold water. Stir into hot milk. Let cool to 110°. Add 1 c. plain yogurt and stir well. Put lid on kettle; set kettle in large bowl of 110° water. Cover all with thick towel. Let set 4 hours. Take out enough starter (1 c.) for next time. Add flavoring, fruit, and preferred sweetener. Beat well and chill before serving.

Note: Do not add starter to milk hotter than 110°.

—*Mrs. Mervin H. Yoder, Pleasant Hill, IL*

Simple Yogurt

1 gal. whole milk   **1 pt. plain yogurt**

In a 6-qt. kettle, heat milk to 180° then let cool to 125°. In a bowl, mix the pint plain yogurt and a quart of the warm milk. Beat with a wire whip until smooth then pour into the rest of the milk and stir well. Pour into 4 qt. jars and 1 pt. jar. Put in oven with just pilot light on or on top of woodstove shelf for 8 hours. Save the pint for your next batch.

—*Mrs. Raymond Yutzy, Howe, IN*

Homemade Cultured Buttermilk

2 c. skim or whole milk or buttermilk
2 Tbsp. commercial buttermilk

Mix well. Let stand 16-24 hours in a warm place until thickened. Refrigerate. Before using, shake well or blend in blender to produce the classical texture. Keeps 2 weeks in the refrigerator. Use all but 2 Tbsp., then add more milk and repeat ripening procedure to replenish.

—Charlene Kennell, South Wayne, WI

Homemade Sour Cream

After making your own yogurt and buttermilk, making sour cream is rather easy! Take equal amounts of buttermilk and yogurt, line a colander with a non-fuzzy cloth (flour sack towels are great), pour in, and let drain for 6-24 hours, however thick you want it. Milk can be added if it gets too thick.

—Mrs. Susan Schwartz, Mt. Perry, OH

Yogurt Cream Cheese

Put yogurt in a cheesecloth bag. Hang the bag on the kitchen faucet and let drain overnight or until yogurt is the consistency of cream cheese. For sharper cheese, use yogurt that is several days old. Salt if desired. Yield: 1 qt. makes 8 oz. cream cheese.

—Erma Hoover, Penn Yan, NY

Experience is the best teacher.

Cream Cheese

Into one gallon whole milk (room temperature) pour 1 packet kefir starter culture and mix well. Incubate at about 85° for 12 hours. Pour into cheesecloth-lined colander and drain off the whey. Drain until it's the consistency of cream cheese. If you want to use it as cottage cheese, just don't drain it as long.

—*Alice Wilkerson, Fordland, MO*

Cream Cheese

3¼ c. whole milk
2¾ c. whipping cream
2 drops liquid rennet

½ tsp. mesophilic powdered starter

Put the milk and cream in a double boiler and blend with a whisk. Heat to barely 72°. Remove from heat and sprinkle starter on surface and gently whisk to blend. Add rennet and gently blend. Cover and let ripen 24-26 hours at room temperature. Line a colander with cheesecloth and pour curds into colander. Knot the ends of the cloth and put the handle of a wooden spoon under the knot. Hang it over a pot and let drain another 12 hours until whey ceases to run. Spoon the curds into a bowl and press down a bit. Refrigerate before using.

—*Mrs. Raymond Yutzy, Howe, IN*

It is quite possible to improve your disposition, increase your efficiency, and change your personality for the better. The way to do it is to avoid cane and beet sugar in all forms and guises.

—*John W. Tintera*

One tablespoon sulfur put in stove will almost instantly stop the worst stovepipe or chimney fire. If a tablespoon of sulfur is put in the stove every week, the pipes will rarely have to be taken down to clean.

When heating goats' milk, heat as rapidly as possible without burning. It tends to have more of a 'goaty' taste when heated slowly. Also be sure to use fresh milk.

Wash seedless grapes, dry on a towel, then put in baggies and freeze. I also do that with blueberries. It makes a delicious treat for children instead of giving them candy.

Don't know what to give the married children for Christmas? Buy a wicker basket at a Dollar General for $3-$5. Fill up with oranges, grapefruit, bananas, grapes, or whatever fresh fruits and vegetables you want. A hunk of cheese and a loaf of bread can be put in too. Tuck a pair or two of gloves in if there are little children who always keep "losing" theirs. Use your imagination.

Adding alcohol to window washing in the winter will make that the windows don't freeze as fast as you wash them off.

To remove mildew stains, soak the piece 15-20 minutes in a solution of ¼ to ⅓ c. bleaching agent and about ½ c. of vinegar to 2 qt. water. Never hurts color fast. It works!

Too expensive to buy clothes hampers for every child's room? Just buy a waste can without a lid at a discount or Dollar General store. If you only wash what's in the basket, they'll soon learn to pitch their clothes in. Then before taking the empty cans back in their rooms, I pitch each one's socks in as I fold them.

Candy

Peanut Butter Confection

½ c. peanut butter
1 c. powdered milk
½ c. molasses or honey

½ c. raisins
1 Tbsp. nutritional yeast

Mix all ingredients well with hands, kneading to pie dough consistency. Roll into balls and chill.

—*Elizabeth Mullet, Pantego, NC*

Horehound Candy

1 c. fresh horehound or
½ c. dried

1 qt. lemon juice
3 lb. honey

Simmer horehound in lemon juice for 20 minutes; strain. Combine honey and horehound mixture. Boil to hard crack. Pour into buttered pans and let cool completely. Crack into pieces by hitting it with the end of a table knife.

—*Laura Royer, Camden, IN*

Pecan Crumbles

½ c. butter
1½ c. maple syrup

3½ c. pecans, chopped

Melt butter in an iron skillet. Add maple syrup and cook for 10 minutes, stirring frequently. Add pecans. Continue cooking for 15 minutes. Very good over ice cream or in granola or as a snack.

—*Mrs. Johnny Miller, Loudonville, OH*

Old-Fashioned Sorghum Candy

¼ c. butter
2 c. sorghum
1 tsp. vanilla

1 tsp. vinegar
½ tsp. soda

Stir butter and sorghum over slow heat until butter is melted. Then boil slowly to the hard ball stage (265°). Syrup should become brittle when dropped in cold water. Stir the syrup as it thickens. Add vanilla, vinegar, and soda. Pour onto buttered platter. Lightly flour the hands and pull as soon as candy can be handled. Pull until it becomes light in color, twist, and cut into pieces.

Note: Always boil sorghum candy syrup slowly so as not to burn it.

—*Jolene Bontrager, Hillsboro, WI*

Super Fudge

1 c. honey
1 c. peanut butter
1 c. carob powder
1 c. sesame seeds

½ c. coconut
1 c. sunflower seeds
½ c. dates or other dried fruit

Heat the honey and peanut butter until melted, then add carob powder. Mix well. Add rest of ingredients. Mix well again, then press into greased pan. Refrigerate to harden. Keep refrigerated.

—*Mary Showalter, Mt. Solon, VA*

A Bible that is falling apart probably belongs to someone who isn't.

Peanut Butter Candy

1 c. honey
1 c. peanut butter

1 c. powdered milk
½ c. sesame seeds

Mix all together and knead. Then shape into balls.

—Mary E. Showalter, Mt. Solon, VA

Maple Syrup-N-Peanut Butter Candy

2½ c. maple syrup
1 Tbsp. butter

⅔ c. cream
⅓ c. peanut butter

Cook maple syrup, butter, and cream until hard ball stage (265°). Take off from heat and stir in ⅓ c. peanut butter. Keep on stirring candy until it has changed color and wants to thicken. Pour quickly into a greased cake pan (preferably a glass pan). Work quickly in spreading it out as it hardens almost immediately. Let cool, cut, and eat.

—Jolene Bontrager, Hillsboro, WI

Honey Peanut Brittle

1 c. honey
¼ c. butter

2 c. raw peanuts
1 tsp. baking soda

In a 2-qt. saucepan, combine honey and butter. Boil slowly. When candy thermometer reaches 280°, add peanuts. Continue boiling until thermometer registers 300°. Remove from heat. Quickly stir in soda. Pour on buttered baking sheet. Cool, then break in pieces.

—Mary S. Yoder, Wooster, OH

Maple Cream

1 gal. maple syrup

Boil in a 12-qt. kettle to soft ball stage. Watch continually as it can boil over quickly. Cool to warm; stir. As it thickens add more maple syrup until it has a nice spreading consistency. Best spread on homemade bread.

—*Mary Margaret Hochstetler, Milford, IN*

Maple Spread

In a large saucepan, bring maple syrup to a boil; add ½ tsp. butter to keep it from boiling over. Boil to 232°. Remove from heat and set in a cool, quiet place till room temperature. Stir till it turns a lighter color; this takes around ½ hour. Pour quickly into small containers. Keep refrigerated.

—*Elizabeth Drudge, Wroxeter, Ontario*

Caramel Popcorn

½ c. popping corn	⅓ c. water
1¾ c. honey	¼ tsp. salt
¼ c. butter	

Pop the popping corn. Set aside. Grease cookie sheets. Combine remaining ingredients in a saucepan and bring to a boil over medium heat, stirring continuously. Continue cooking, stirring occasionally, until mixture reaches 280°. Pour caramel mixture over popcorn; stir until well coated. Spread on greased cookie sheets to cool.

Note: To make popcorn balls, grease your hands and form mixture into balls while warm. Wrap in waxed paper to cool.

—*Laura Yoder, Free Union, VA*

Popcorn Crunch

½ c. butter, melted   3 qt. popped corn
½ c. honey   1 c. nuts, chopped
1 tsp. cinnamon

Blend butter, honey, and cinnamon. Heat until well blended. Pour over popcorn/nut mixture. Mix well. Spread over cookie sheet in thin layer. Bake at 350° for 10-15 minutes or until crisp.

Variation: 2 Tbsp. peanut butter can be used and also sorghum can be used instead of honey.

—*Laura Royer, Camden, IN*

Living
Slow down, exit the rat race
Take time to lie under a tree
And watch the clouds
Moving across the sky
Go out at night
And name the stars
Take a walk in the woods
Along the riverbank
Watch for wildlife
Identify the trees
Find a pretty flower
Visit with friends
Play with a child
Help a neighbor
Remember what life is all about
Live, love, and prepare for eternity.
—RY

Seasonings & Mixes

The Salt of the Earth

Even though many people have been advised to limit their salt intake, we do need salt. How much we need varies from person to person. People who eat mainly raw foods do not need as much salt. People who eat mostly cooked foods need more salt to activate digestive enzymes in the intestine. Someone who has weak adrenal glands should eat plenty of salt. In some cases, salt has helped reduce high blood pressure.

Let us look at how our salt is processed. Most people do not realize that our salt is highly refined – just like our flour, sugar, and oils. The table salt we use and even most so-called sea salt has been heated to 2,000° and stripped of all its magnesium and trace minerals. Additives such as aluminum silicate are used to make it free flowing. It is then bleached to make it white. Ironically, some of the minerals stripped from the salt are bought by nutritional companies, then sold to the public as health supplements. So we see that even though we need salt, we are not getting the right kind if we buy the highly processed kind that is so readily available at the grocery stores, because this kind of salt can be harmful to our health.

Celtic sea salt is an excellent choice of salt to use. This kind is made by sun-drying the salt water of the ocean. The finished product contains over 70 trace minerals and the natural iodine our bodies need.

Another good kind to use is Real salt. Real salt is mined naturally and contains iodine and over 50 other trace minerals. (See sources.)

Can that which is unsavoury be eaten without salt? or is there any taste in the white of an egg?
—Job 6:6
Ye are the salt of the earth: but if the salt have lost his savour, wherewith shall it be salted? it is thenceforth good for nothing, but to be cast out, and to be trodden under foot of men.
—Matthew 5:13

Salt Substitute

3 bay leaves, broken
  into pieces
3 tsp. dried minced onion
2 tsp. dried rosemary, crushed
1 tsp. garlic powder

1 tsp. dried marjoram
1 tsp. rubbed sage
1 tsp. dried thyme
½ tsp. lemon-pepper seasoning
½ tsp. pepper

Place all ingredients into a blender, cover, and process until finely ground. Transfer to a salt shaker and use in place of salt.

—Mrs. Leroy B. Miller, Middlefield, OH

No-Salt Seasoning

1 Tbsp. onion powder
1 Tbsp. garlic powder
1 Tbsp. paprika
1 tsp. thyme
1 tsp. oregano
½ tsp. pepper

½ tsp. celery seed
⅛ tsp. cayenne pepper
2 tsp. parsley flakes
½ tsp. cumin
1 tsp. basil

Combine all ingredients in a small jar with a shaker top. Use for seasoning fish, poultry, vegetables, stews, and soups. Yield: about 2 oz.

—Cyndi Davis, Flemingsburg, KY

Real, unrefined salt from ancient seabeds was highly prized by people of long ago. Salt was sometimes used as a means of exchange instead of money.

Chicken-Style Seasoning

3 c. Nutritional Yeast (yellow in color)
7 tsp. dry bell pepper or dry vegetable flakes
3½ tsp. salt
2½ tsp. celery salt
4½ tsp. garlic powder
3 Tbsp. onion powder
9 Tbsp. parsley flakes
4½ tsp. thyme, optional
2¼ tsp. marjoram, optional

Grind all ingredients together in blender and store in tightly covered container. You have to use a little more than regular chicken base, but is so much better for you.

—*Mrs. Joni Troyer, Millersburg, OH*

Herb Scasoning

¼ c. dried parsley
¼ c. dried leaf chervil
¼ c. freeze-dried chives
¼ c. leaf tarragon

Combine herbs in a shaker. Use for soups, fish, gravy, dressings, and vegetables.

—*Miriam Hershberger, Middlefield, OH*

Italian Herb Mix

1 tsp. dried oregano
1 tsp. dried basil
1 tsp. dried marjoram

Mix together and store in an airtight container.

—*Marie Raber, Baltic, OH*

Taco Seasoning Mix

1 tsp. chili powder
1 tsp. paprika
1½ tsp. cumin
2 tsp. parsley flakes

1 tsp. onion powder
½ tsp. garlic salt
½ tsp. oregano

Mix all together. This is the equivalent of one package from the store.

—Mrs. Naomi Ruth Bontrager, Mio, MI

Homemade Taco Seasoning

5 Tbsp. chili powder
3 Tbsp. dried oregano
3 Tbsp. cornstarch
2 Tbsp. dried basil

2 Tbsp. crushed cayenne
   pepper flakes or 1 Tbsp.
   ground cayenne
2 Tbsp. garlic powder

Mix together well. Store in airtight container. Use 1½-2½ Tbsp. to flavor 1 lb. of browned ground beef. Add ½-¾ c. water and simmer until thickened. Serve in your favorite tacos or taco salad recipe.

—Charlene Kennell, South Wayne, WI

Pumpkin Pie Spice

1 tsp. cinnamon
⅓ tsp. cloves

⅓ tsp. nutmeg
⅓ tsp. allspice

—Mrs. Naomi Ruth Bontrager, Mio, MI

Graham Cracker Crust Substitute

1 c. wheat germ
1 Tbsp. honey

¼ c. oil
½ tsp. cinnamon

Stir together well. Press into pan. Chill and proceed with desired recipe.

—*Charlene Kennell, South Wayne, WI*

Pancake and Bisquick® Mix

8 c. wheat flour
⅓ c. baking powder

2 tsp. salt
2 tsp. cream of tartar

Mix together and store in airtight container. For pancakes and Bisquick®, add 1 egg to ¾ c. mix, ½ Tbsp. oil, and enough milk to make the right consistency.

—*Wilma Schmucker, Mio, MI*

Gluten-Free Flour Mix

6 c. rice flour
2 c. potato starch

1 c. tapioca starch
1 tsp. xanthum gum, optional

Mix very thoroughly. Use in most gluten-free recipes. Tastes much better than plain rice flour.

—*Miriam Schrock, Rutherford, TN*

> *The fairest thing in nature, a flower, still*
> *has its roots in earth and manure.*
> —*D. H. Lawrence*

Crumbs for Canned Chicken

2 c. graham flour
1 c. cornmeal
½ c. wheat germ
2 Tbsp. salt
½ tsp. black pepper

1 tsp. basil leaves, crushed
½ tsp. curry powder
1 tsp. garlic salt
½ c. olive oil

Mix all ingredients well. Store in container with tight-fitting lid in refrigerator. Remove amount needed. Drain canned chicken. Dip pieces in milk; roll in coating. Place in baking pan in single layer. Bake at 375° till browned.

—*Mrs. Allen A. Bontrager, LaGrange, IN*

Homemade Baking Powder

2 c. arrowroot powder
2 c. cream of tartar

1 c. soda

Sift together several times until well blended. Use as any other baking powder.

—*Mrs. Urie R. Miller, Shipshewana, IN*

Baking Powder

2 Tbsp. cream of tartar
1 Tbsp. baking soda

1 Tbsp. cornstarch

Sift three times. Yield: ¼ c.

—*Mary E. Beachy, Liberty, KY*

Egg Substitute

½ tsp. baking powder   2 Tbsp. milk

Equals 1 egg. Works well in any cake or cookie recipe.

—*Mrs. Naomi Ruth Bontrager, Mio, MI*

Egg Substitute

Add ½ c. ground flaxseed to 1½ c. cold water in a small sauce-pan. Bring to a boil; stir constantly. Boil 3 minutes. Cool. Keep in a closed jar in refrigerator and use in baking recipes, substituting 1 Tbsp. for every egg.

—*Mrs. Naomi Ruth Bontrager, Mio, MI*

Homemade Vanilla Extract

2 vanilla beans   1 oz. alcohol (Use vodka,
                              rum, brandy, or cognac)

Slit beans lengthwise to expose inner seeds. Place beans in al-cohol in glass jar. Let set 2-3 weeks. Strain.

—*Mrs. Leroy B. Miller, Middlefield, OH*

Better is a dinner of herbs where love is,
than a stalled ox and hatred therewith.
—*Proverbs 15:17*

Homemade Vinegar

Set a gallon of fresh cider in a warm dark place without a cap on the jug. Place a cloth over the opening and secure cloth with a rubber band to keep out dirt. Let set for 7 weeks. If it doesn't seem quite finished, let it set a while longer. If it forms a film on top of it, take that off. You can strain it too.

—Mrs. Naomi Ruth Bontrager, Mio, MI

Healthy Baby Food

½ c. water
⅛ c. brown rice flour
(coarse setting)

7 drops Calcium &
Magnesium (Bedtime)
7 drops extra-virgin olive oil

Mix part of the water with flour, dissolve, bring rest of water to a boil, and add flour mixture. Stir rapidly till thick. Add drops. Some chopped apples may be added.

—Ruth Wanner, Conneautville, PA

Coating for Pans

½ c. coconut oil, softened
or melted

¼ c. whole wheat flour

Mix oil with flour to form a smooth mixture. Keep in a covered dish at room temperature so it stays soft. It will stay sweet and soft indefinitely. Use for greasing cake pans, muffin pans, etc. Using a brush works best.

—Mrs. Abie J. Troyer, Ashland, OH

A quick way to get rid of paint smell...cut up onions and lay around in room where painting. Do not use onions for food afterwards as they are full of paint poison...or cook a little vinegar or tomato juice in a kettle on stove while painting.

Something to remember when baking with whole grains and natural sweeteners – the finished product will spoil quicker than when using enriched, refined ingredients.

When boiling meat on the bones for broth, letting the broth cool several hours or overnight with the bones still in it, will result in a firmer gelled broth. The broth may be reheated to melt it, if necessary, to take out the bones.

When cooking fresh eggs, crack each one a little bit before putting in kettle; they will peel like old eggs.

Vinegar rubbed over moldy cheese makes the mold disappear and no waste of cheese. This works for almost anything to get rid of mold.

¾ c. honey and ¼ c. vinegar mixed together gets rid of cataracts and many eye problems. Rub over the eyes and blink a few times. Do this 3 or so times daily. Do for 3 weeks to see the difference in eyesight.

Myrrh tea (1 tsp. per qt.) will take away yeast infection, thrush in babies' mouth, canker sores, and sores in mouth. Adults should drink 1 qt. a day, children 2 c.

Canning & Freezing

Sugarfree Apple Butter

2 gal. applesauce	1 tsp. cloves
3 qt. grape concentrate	1 tsp. allspice
2 tsp. cinnamon	1 tsp. salt

Cook applesauce and grape concentrate slowly until desired thickness, about 3-4 hours. Use heavy stockpot and stir often. When thick enough take out 1 c. and add spices. Blend together, then pour back into stockpot and mix well. Pour into hot sterile jars and seal.

—*Mrs. Junior Detweiler, Redding, IA*

Sugarless Apple Butter

1 gallon cider – preferably made with sweet apples like Yellow Delicious

1 gallon applesauce – I can Yellow Delicious apples with no sugar and use this

Cover stove with foil before starting. Cook cider down to half-ways at least, then add applesauce and cook till thickness of apple butter you prefer. Stir more often once sauce is added. Pour all together in one container before adding some cinnamon and/ or cloves, unless you prefer it without. Put in jars and process in boiling water bath 15 minutes.

—*Mrs. Andy E. N. Yoder, Millersburg, OH*

> *Man doesn't live by bread alone; he*
> *needs buttering up once in a while.*

Apple Pie Filling

20 c. water
7 c. arrowroot powder
1 c. flour
2 Tbsp. nutmeg
3 Tbsp. cinnamon

3 tsp. stevia or 4 c. maple
 syrup
¼ c. honey
1 Tbsp. salt

Cook together. Add 1 bu. apples, peeled and diced. Stuff into jars and process 20 minutes in hot water bath.

Variation: You can also substitute blueberries for apples. Omit spices and add 1 c. lemon juice and just a touch of nutmeg. Experiment with pineapple juice also, to be used as part of the water.

—*Mrs. John Houston, Cottage Grove, TN*

Apple Pie Filling to Can (Apple Schnitz)

2 tsp. stevia
3 Tbsp. honey, optional
2 Tbsp. nutmeg
3 Tbsp. cinnamon

½ Tbsp. salt
4 c. flour
1 bu. apples, peeled and
 diced

Mix dry ingredients and toss with apples. Put into jars and hot water bath for 25 minutes.

—*Mrs. John Houston, Cottage Grove, TN*

Freezing Strawberries

Mash ripe berries. Sprinkle 13-qt. bowlful with ½ tsp. stevia. Add 1 Tbsp. maple syrup. Mix well. Freeze.

—*Mrs. John Houston, Cottage Grove, TN*

To Can Peaches or Pears Without Sugar

Slice fruit and pack into jars as full as possible. Pour into jars until full to the neck: orange juice, grape juice, apple juice, or pineapple juice. These juices should be pure with no sugar in them. These fruits are very tasty like this. The juices help to sweeten the fruit. Process in hot water bath, letting it boil for 5 minutes.

—*Mary Eicher, Quincy, MI*

Canning Peaches with Stevia

Wash fresh peaches with a fruit wash to get spray off. Rinse. Peel peaches and cut in desired sizes. Put into qt. jars. Put 12 drops (or to suit taste) stevia extract into each quart jar. Fill with water. Cold pack for 10 minutes.

—*Mrs. Crist Yoder, Baltic, OH*

Fruit Cocktail

1 bu. Baby Gold peaches	Syrup:
1 bu. pears	46 oz. pineapple juice
2 gal. tidbit pineapple	1 gal. water
8 lbs. white grapes	1 tsp. stevia
	1 tsp. vanilla

Peel and dice peaches and pears. Mix with rest of fruit. Pack into jars. Mix syrup ingredients and pour over fruit in jars. Put on lids and process in hot water bath 20 minutes.

To can pears: Pare and dice pears. Fill jars and use syrup recipe above. Process in hot water bath 10 minutes.

—*Mrs. John Houston, Cottage Grove, TN*

To Can Cider

In a large pot heat cider to 180°. Hold at that temperature for 10 minutes. Ladle into hot jars and screw on lids. Place upside down to seal. This tastes like fresh cider.

—Mrs. Raymond Yutzy, Howe, IN

Dorothy's Ketchup

5 qt. tomato juice	1 tsp. cinnamon
2 onions	1 tsp. nutmeg
2 tsp. stevia	1 tsp. ginger
2 Tbsp. honey	½ tsp. allspice
1 c. vinegar	½ tsp. red pepper
¼ c. salt	½ c. arrowroot powder

Put through blender and liquefy everything. Pour into large kettle and cook 1½ hours. Put in jars and hot water bath for 10 minutes.

—Mrs. John Houston, Cottage Grove, TN

Ketchup

2 gal. tomato pulp (tomato juice that has been drained in cloth bag)	½ tsp. onion salt
	1 tsp. celery salt
	¼ tsp. cinnamon
2 c. honey	⅛ tsp. cloves
½ tsp. mustard powder	1 Tbsp. taco seasoning
¼ c. salt (less if salt in juice)	½ c. clear jel, optional
1 c. vinegar	

Put all together in a big kettle over heat until it boils. Put in jars and process 10 minutes. Yield: approximately 10 pt.

—Jolene Bontrager, Hillsboro, WI

Homemade Catsup

3 gal. unpeeled tomatoes,
  chopped
6 onions, chopped
9 peach leaves, optional
6 sweet red peppers
2 c. carrots, chopped
2 red beets, chopped
2 hot peppers, seeded
1 c. basil leaves, optional
½ c. oregano leaves, optional
2 cloves garlic, optional
¼ tsp. cinnamon
½ tsp. cloves
½ tsp. mustard
1½ c. vinegar
1 c. honey
1½ Tbsp. salt

Boil the first 10 ingredients 45 minutes or till soft, stirring often. Drain off juice. Put pulp through blender and then through Victorio Strainer. Add seasonings and rest of ingredients and cook 1 more hour. Bottle and seal.

—*Mary E. Showalter, Mt. Solon, VA*

Delicious Salsa

½ bu. tomatoes
5 hot peppers
5 green peppers
3 lb. onions, chopped
10 – 6 oz. cans tomato paste
1 whole large head garlic,
  diced
4 medium hot peppers
¼ c. honey
5 Tbsp. salt
⅔ c. vinegar
1 tsp. garlic powder
1 tsp. paprika
½ c. parsley flakes
7 Tbsp. clear jel
¾ c. water

Cook tomatoes, garlic, and peppers together 1 hour. Add rest of ingredients except clear jel and water and cook 45 minutes. Mix clear jel with water, add, and boil 1 minute. Fill jars. Cold pack 20 minutes. I use this to make pizza and is better than pizza sauce.

—*Mary Detweiler, West Farmington, OH*

Crisp Dilled Beans

2 lb. small green beans
1 tsp. red pepper
4 cloves garlic
4 large heads dill

2 c. water
¼ c. salt
1 pt. vinegar

Stem beans and pack lengthwise in hot jars. To each pint add ¼ tsp. red pepper or 1 fresh chili pepper, 1 clove garlic, and 1 head dill. Heat water, salt, and vinegar. Bring to a boil; pour over beans. Put lids on at once. Process in boiling water bath for 5 minutes. Yield: 4 pt.

—*Amelia Troyer, Glenford, OH*

Richard Martin's Jalapeño Peppers

1 c. vinegar
¼ c. water
¼ c. olive oil

1 tsp. salt
1 tsp. pickling spices

Wash peppers and pack tightly into jars. Heat all ingredients to boiling. Pour over peppers to 1" from top of jar. Put on cap, screw on firm tight. Process 10 minutes in boiling water bath.

Note: If you oil your hands and wear rubber gloves or plastic bags when cutting bigger peppers into smaller pieces, you might save your hands from burning.

—*Jean Pichiya, Liberty, PA*

> *When the only tool you have is a hammer,*
> *all problems begin to resemble nails.*
> —*Abraham Maslow*

251

Sandwich Peppers

½ bu. medium hot peppers   1 Tbsp. salt per quart
1 large head dill per quart   1 cherry pepper per quart
3 cloves garlic per quart   4 qt. vinegar
2 Tbsp. mustard seed per quart   8 qt. water

Put dill, garlic, mustard seed, salt, and cherry pepper in each jar. Cut peppers lengthwise to fit sandwich and fill jar tightly with peppers. Put filled jars in 200° oven until hot. Heat vinegar and water and pour hot over peppers. Put hot lid on and invert jars 15-20 minutes then turn upright. Do not water bath.

—Mary Detweiler, West Farmington, OH

Mock Olive Dill Peppers

1 qt. cold water   1 pt. vinegar
¾ c. salt

Cut sweet bell peppers into strips and put in jars. Boil water, salt, and vinegar. Put in jars, hot or cold. Process in hot water bath until almost boiling.

—Miss Betty Hilty, Oakfield, ME

Delicious Dill Pickles

1 qt. water   ¾ c. maple syrup or ½ c. honey
1 c. vinegar   4 tsp. salt

Mix all together and bring to boiling. Pack sliced pickles into jars. Also to each quart jar add a slice of onion, 2 large garlic cloves, and a few dill sprigs. Pour boiling mixture over pickles. Enough for 8 qt. Put in hot water bath. Bring to a boil, then turn off heat and let set for 10 minutes.

—Mary Nolt, Withee, WI

Dill Pickles

6 c. water	dill
3 c. apple cider vinegar	garlic cloves
½ c. salt	red pepper

To each quart put 1 head dill or 1 Tbsp. dill, 3 cloves garlic, and several shakes red pepper. Then place pickles in jar. Heat water, vinegar, and salt to boiling hot and pour over pickles. Put on lids and water bath for 5 minutes.

Note: Some don't care for quite this much vinegar. You could cut it back.

—*Laura Royer, Camden, IN*

Okra Pickles

3½ lb. okra pods	⅓ c. salt
1 pt. vinegar	3 small hot peppers, optional
1 qt. water	2 tsp. dill seeds
garlic bud	

Pack okra firmly in hot sterilized jars. Put a garlic bud in each jar. Bring rest of ingredients to boil and pour over okra in jars and seal. Process in boiling water bath at simmering temperature about 180°-200° for 10 minutes. Let ripen several weeks before opening.

—*Mary Showalter, Mt. Solon, VA*

Most things that make us sigh and fret
are things that haven't happened yet.

Pickled Red Beets

2 c. red beet juice	1 Tbsp. salt
1 c. vinegar	½ cinnamon stick
¾ c. honey	3 whole cloves

Mix all together and bring to boil. Let set for a while then take out cinnamon and cloves. Cook beets until tender. Peel, slice, and put in jars. Pour syrup over beets. Cold pack 15-20 minutes. Beet juice comes from the water you use to cook the beets in, so make sure the beets are scrubbed clean before you cook them!

—*Mary Fisher, Rebersburg, PA*

Pickled Red Beet Brine

1 qt. water	4 tsp. salt
2 c. vinegar	1 tsp. cinnamon, optional
1 c. maple syrup or ½ c. honey	

Combine all ingredients and bring to boil. Pack cut-up cooked beets in jars. Cover with boiled brine. Hot water bath for 5 minutes. Yield: enough for 8 qt.

—*Mary Nolt, Withee, WI*

Coleslaw to Can

1 large head cabbage, shredded	½ c. celery, chopped
¾ c. carrots, shredded	½ c. vinegar
2 tsp. salt	½ c. onion, chopped
¾ c. honey	½ tsp. celery seed
	½ tsp. mustard seed

Mix together, then put into jars. Process in hot water bath for 10 minutes.

—*Erma Hoover, Penn Yan, NY*

Bean and Bacon Soup to Can

4 qt. tomato cocktail	1 pt. pizza sauce
5 qt. tomato juice	6 tsp. salt
1 lb. beans	2 tsp. pepper
2 lb. bacon, cut up and fried	1 tsp. onion salt
1 large onion, chopped	½ tsp. garlic powder
2 c. celery, chopped	1 qt. water
2 c. potatoes, chopped	

Soak beans overnight. Then cook till almost soft. Fry onion in bacon grease. You can mash or put through blender 2½ c. of the beans to thicken the soup. Mix everything together and simmer for ½ hour. Put in jars and pressure cook for 1 hour at 10 lbs. Yield: 14 qt.

—Ruth Wanner, Conneautville, PA

Bean and Bacon Soup

4 lb. navy beans	2 bay leaves
2 lb. bacon	4 qt. tomato juice
6 c. onion, chopped	4 c. carrots, diced
4-6 c. celery, chopped	8 c. potatoes, diced
2 tsp. pepper	salt to taste

Soak beans overnight, then cook until soft. Cook celery, carrots, and potatoes until soft. Cut bacon finely and fry. Remove from pan and add onion to bacon grease. Fry until tender. Put all ingredients together in large canner and heat until it simmers. Remove bay leaves before putting soup into jars. Can 1 hour at 10 lb. in pressure cooker. Yield: approximately 16 qt.

—Amanda Bricker, Cass City, MI

Hamburger Vegetable Soup

1 qt. potatoes
1 qt. carrots
1 qt. navy beans
1 qt. peas
1 qt. corn
1 qt. onions
2 c. brown rice cooked in 5-6 c. salt water

6-7 qt. tomato juice
¼-½ c. honey or sorghum
3 lb. hamburger
2 Tbsp. chili powder
salt to taste

Cook vegetables separately with salt, but not quite soft. Fry meat in butter and add seasonings. Mix all together, put in jars, and cold pack 2 hours.

—*Mrs. Esther Yoder, Hillsboro, WI*

Vegetable Soup

5 qt. potatoes, diced
5 qt. corn
5 qt. navy beans
3 qt. peas
3 qt. kidney beans
2 qt. carrots, diced
2 qt. celery, diced
1 lb. barley

2 qt. green beans
6 qt. tomato juice
1 gal. whole tomatoes, cut
   up finely
12 lbs. hamburger, fried
   and seasoned
salt to taste
5 large onions

Precook all vegetables and barley separately except onions. Drain all vegetables except potatoes. Add potato water to soup. Mix all together. Add water for more liquid. Put in jars and process in boiling water for 3 hours. Yield: approximately 40 qt.

—*Miss Betty Hilty, Oakfield, ME*

Vegetable Soup to Can

2 c. brown rice
1 qt. water
1 lb. pinto beans
1 lb. lentils
1 lb. navy beans
1 lb. black-eyed peas
2 large onions, chopped
2 c. celery with greens and
   tops
6 large carrots, sliced

2 qt. beef broth with meat
1 lb. frozen lima beans
6 c. frozen corn
1 lb. frozen peas
6 c. green beans
2 medium-large zucchini,
   diced
6 c. cauliflower
6 c. broccoli
1-2 qt. tomato juice

Cook rice in water till rice swells. Put dried beans, lentils, and peas in kettle, cover with water, and cook for 10 minutes. Cook to thaw frozen vegetables. Mix all together and put into jars. To each jar add 1 slice pepper and 1 tsp. salt per quart. Pressure pints for 40 minutes at 10 lbs. Quarts for 45 minutes at 10 lbs. This recipe is very interchangeable. Any grains can be used; barley is good. Some vegetables can be omitted.

—*Carol Hostetler, Doylesburg, PA*

Chili Soup to Can

5 lb. hamburger
2 c. onions, chopped
salt and pepper
1 gal. cooked dark red kidney
   beans
1 gal. tomato juice

1 c. sorghum
1 c. pickle relish
1 tsp. garlic salt
2 Tbsp. chili powder
1 qt. water

Brown hamburger with onions, salt, and pepper. In a large stockpot, heat the rest of ingredients. Add hamburger mixture. Heat through. Put in jars and cold pack 3 hours.

—*Mrs. J. T., Hestand, KY*

Chili Soup to Can

6 qt. tomato juice	3 Tbsp. garlic salt
3 qt. water	3 Tbsp. spike
3 qt. cooked Northern beans	3 Tbsp. chili powder
8 lb. hamburger	3 Tbsp. parsley flakes
2 large onions, chopped	

Fry hamburger and onions. Mix all ingredients together. Pour into cans. Pressure can at 10 lb. for 45 minutes.

—*Mrs. Raymond Yutzy, Howe, IN*

Lena Mae's Chicken Noodle Soup to Can

2 qt. potatoes, diced	1 Tbsp. salt
2 qt. carrots, diced	1 gal. noodles
2 qt. celery, chopped	4 chickens, cooked and
1 c. onion, chopped	deboned

Cook veggies and noodles in chicken broth. Add chicken meat. Mix all together, put in jars, and cold pack 3 hours or pressure cook 10 lb. for 75 minutes. When ready to use, empty jars into kettle; add 1 qt. water and 2 Tbsp. chicken soup base (with no MSG).

—*Mrs. John Houston, Cottage Grove, TN*

> *Let us cease pretending that toothbrushes and toothpaste are any more important than shoe brushes and shoe polish. It is store food that has given us store teeth.*
>
> —*Earnest Hooten*

Chicken Soup Mixture to Can

In each pint jar put ½ c. cooked chicken pieces. Add the following in layers of several Tbsp. each: diced potatoes, diced carrots, chopped celery. Add 1 tsp. minced onion and parsley, plus ½ tsp. salt, a dash of cayenne pepper, and 1 tsp. chicken soup base. Fill jars with chicken broth or water. Pressure can at 10 lb. for ½ hour (or according to manufacturer's instructions for your pressure cooker).

To serve: Heat mixture with equal amount of water and several Tbsp. rice or noodles or desired additions. Simmer until rice is fully cooked. This mixture is widely variable for many different soups and casseroles. Use your own imagination and ideas to create delicious meals with it.

—Amanda Bricker, Cass City, MI

Mixed Vegetables to Can

carrots, shredded
celery, chopped

onions, chopped
potatoes, shredded

Layer in jars. Fill with carrots, celery, and onions to a little over halfway, then fill up with potatoes. Do not pack tightly. Add 1 tsp. salt to each jar and fill with water up to neck of jar. Pressure can for 40 minutes at 10 lb. pressure. Nice to have on hand to add to chicken noodle soup, dressing, casseroles, and bean soups. You can wash the small new potatoes in the washing machine and shred them with the peelings still on.

—Mrs. Mervin Yoder, Pleasant Hill, IL

*By spending more for better food, you save
in the long run by saving your health.*

Barbecue Beef Patties to Can

15 lb. hamburger	72 crackers, finely crushed
4 eggs, beaten	6 c. milk
4 slices whole wheat bread	¼ c. salt
2 c. oatmeal	2 Tbsp. pepper

Mix all together, shape into small patties, and brown in butter in skillet. Or put on cookie sheets and bake in oven until browned. Divide into 14 wide-mouth qt. jars and fill half full with sauce.

Sauce:

1½ qt. ketchup	1 Tbsp. of your favorite
3 medium onions, chopped	seasoning salt
1 Tbsp. (heaping) mustard	1 qt. water
½ c. honey	

Mix well and pour over meat.Can with hot water bath for 2½ hours or pressure cook for 40 minutes at 10 lbs.

—*Mrs. Vernon Hershberger, Loganville,WI*

Canning Venison Chunks

1 tsp. salt	1 tsp. basil
¼ tsp. pepper	1 Tbsp. vinegar

Soak venison chunks in salt water overnight. Drain and fill jars with chunks. To each quart sprinkle on top the above seasonings. Pour a little water on top to wash down the seasonings. Cold pack for 3 hours or pressure cook 1½ hours at 10 lb at 10 lb.

—*Ruth Wanner, Conneautville, PA*

Chicken Burger

24 lb. ground chicken burger
10 Tbsp. salt
1 tsp. cayenne pepper
⅓-½ tsp. garlic powder
½ tsp. ground mustard
½ tsp. poultry seasoning

Add seasonings to chicken burger. Mix well.

—*Mrs. Urie R. Miller, Shipshewana, IN*

Bologna

25 lb. deer meat
5 lb. pork
1½ small bulbs garlic
¾ pt. salt
¼ c. black pepper
1 Tbsp. cumin
½ c. dry mustard
½ c. sage
1½ qt. cornstarch
1 qt. sorghum
2 qt. water

Grind the meat with the garlic. Mix with all the rest of ingredients and grind 2 more times. Stuff into casings and smoke for 3-4 hours or until it is smoked as hard as you want.

Hint: To make wild-tasting deer meat more mild, soak cut-up pieces overnight in 1 pt. vinegar and 1½ pt. salt per 4-5 gal. water. Rinse and drain before grinding.

—*Lydia Hostetler, Danville, OH*

Anyone who is involved with any toxic substance is not working in harmony with the constructive nature of God's plan. To be our brother's keeper means to make sure our brother is cared for, not only financially, but physically, mentally, and spiritually.

—*Dr. Bernard Jensen*

To Mix Sausage

3 Tbsp. salt
¾ Tbsp. black pepper
½ tsp. red pepper

1 tsp. mustard
¾ tsp. sage
1 gal. sausage meat

Can either be mixed before or after grinding. We usually mix it before grinding.

—*Marie Raber, Baltic, OH*

Mincemeat to Can

6 qt. apples, chopped
6 lb. browned sausage
3 qt. sour cherries
1 qt. cider
1 qt. grape juice
4 lb. raisins

5 tsp. salt
1 tsp. cloves
1 Tbsp. cinnamon
1 c. sweetener (or to taste)
½ c. perma flo

Cook apples soft with cider and grape juice, then add raisins and boil a few minutes. Add drained cherries. Mix perma flo with cherry juice and mix well with rest of ingredients. Process pints and quarts 20 minutes at 10 lb. pressure or 1½ hours in boiling water bath. This can also be frozen.
Variation: Hamburger can also be used and more apples if you like.

—*Mrs. Daniel Miller, Homer, MI*

Foolish people who give or sell candy to babies will one day discover, to their horror, that they have much to answer for.
—*Sakurazawa*

Garden Tips

One week before strawberries ripen spray with 2 c. sugar, 2 Tbsp. Maxi crop, and 1 gal. water. The fungus in wet weather will eat the sugar water and let the berries go.

For healthy fruit trees: Around the first of November mix a gallon of wood ashes, 1/3 gal. lime, and 1/3 gal. garden sulfur. Sprinkle around under trees out to drip line. This should do one medium-sized tree. Then take bars of homemade soap and put in a lower fork of tree. One or two per tree, depending on the size of the tree.

Grapevine fertilizer: 1 c. salt, 1 c. lime, and 1 handful bone-meal. Spread around and between plants and hoe it in. Do this in the spring and fall, approximately in March and September. This amount is for each plant.

To ward off tomato hornworms: Sprinkle cornmeal around the plant.

Mix for raspberries: 1 gal. wood ashes, 1 gal. lime, 1 gal. sulfur. Mix together and put a handful to each plant once a month in March, April, and May. Also use dormant spray in March.

Plant Safekeeper cabbage in April or May. When ready in fall take in and wrap each head separately in newspaper. Put in brown paper bags and store in fruit cellar or wherever you store potatoes. You should have cabbage to eat most of the winter.

Add a tablespoon of cornmeal to each pepper and tomato plant and you won't find very many tomato worms, if any.

To prepare a garden or flower bed, put soaked newspapers on top of grass, and add layers of manure, grass clippings, leaves, and peat moss. Cover with plastic until spring; won't need tilling.

NOTES

_____

_____

_____

_____

_____

_____

_____

_____

_____

_____

_____

_____

_____

_____

_____

_____

_____

_____

_____

_____

_____

_____

Soaps & Miscellaneous

All-Purpose Cleaner

¾ c. distilled vinegar
¼ c. borax

1 c. liquid soap
essential oil of your choice

Mix well.

—*Mrs. Reuben Miller, Millersburg, OH*

Laundry Soap

4 lb. lard or 2 lb. lard and
    2 lb. beef tallow
1 – 12 oz. can lye

2 qt. water
½ c. borax
1 c. Basic H (from Shaklee)

Stir lard and lye together real well. Add the water gradually and stir well. Add the soaps and stir till it thickens. Pour out in a cloth-lined container and let set for 1 month before using.

—*Mrs. Ben A. Miller, Smicksburg, PA*

Hand Soap

1 – 12 oz. can lye
3 pt. cold water
5½ lb. clean fat
¼ c. borax
2 c. oatmeal, finely ground

4 oz. Basic H (Shaklee)
2 oz. glycerine
20 drops (more or less)
    essential oil of lavender,
    optional

Pour lye in cold water. When lukewarm add melted fat slowly, stirring with a long-handled paddle or stick. Add the rest of the ingredients and stir 15 minutes. Pour in shallow pans. Cut and let dry out like any other soap.

—*Mrs. Ben A. Miller, Smicksburg, PA*

Toilet Hand Soap

8 c. clean tallow or coconut oil	1 c. boiling water
1 c. lye	2 Tbsp. borax
2 c. cold water	1 tsp. salt

Melt grease; cool. Stir lye into cold water until dissolved. Cool. Dissolve borax and salt in boiling water. Grease a pan (size depends on how thick you want your bars). When grease and lye mixture are same temperature (feel the outside of the container), slowly pour lye water into the grease. Stir often. Add salt solution. When soap is thick like pudding pour into pan. When hard, cut into size bars you want. It is best to let cure a couple months before using. Always use wooden or stainless steel spoons and containers. Plastic pails may also be used. Never aluminum. This is a very nice hard white soap if coconut oil is used. It may also be used as a shampoo. Rub the bar of soap over your wet hair until you have as much as you wish. Rinse with vinegar water.

—*Lydia Hostetler, Danville, OH*

Goat-N-Oat Complexion Soap

1½ qts. goats' milk or unpasteurized, unskimmed cows' milk	6 oz. (½ c. + 2 Tbsp.) lye
	2 c. baby oatmeal
	¼ c. borax
2 lb. unsalted lard or beef tallow	4 oz. glycerine

Work in well ventilated room or outside. Pour milk into mixing bowl. Gently stir lye into milk. It will get very hot. (Careful of fumes!) Stir periodically until mixture cools to 85°. Warm fat until it just melts; maintain 85°-90°. Add borax, glycerine, and oatmeal to the lye/milk mixture, stirring gently. Mix in warm fat. Stir often until it begins to trace. Pour into pan or molds. Let set 24 hours. Cut into bars and remove from pan. Let air-dry for a month. Turn occasionally during curing. Longer curing produces a better product. I like to cure it on a wire. May also be used as shampoo. It might work for dandruff.

—*Mary E. Showalter, Mt. Solon, VA*

Peanut Butter Suet

1 c. peanut butter
2 c. quick oats
2 c. cornmeal

1 c. lard (no substitutes)
1 c. "healthy" flour

Melt lard and peanut butter, then stir in remaining ingredients. Pour into square freezer containers about 1½" thick. Cut to size, separate blocks with waxed paper and store in freezer.

—*Mrs. Andy E. N. Yoder, Millersburg, OH*

Baby Wipes

2 c. boiling water
3 Tbsp. Baby Bath or Basic H (Shaklee)

1 Tbsp. baby oil

Cut a roll of Bounty® paper towels in half. Place half-sized paper towels upright into an airtight container and pour solution over it. Cover tightly. Let set an hour. Now cut an X in your lid. Remove the center cardboard and your wipes may be pulled up through the X from the center of roll like any store-bought ones, at any length. For best results, it's important to use the Bounty® brand.

—*Gertie Troyer, Loganville, WI*

For the Lord thy God bringeth thee into a good land, a land of brooks of water, of fountains and depths that spring out of valleys and hills; A land of wheat, and barley, and vines, and fig trees, and pomegranates; a land of olive oil, and honey.

—*Deuteronomy 8:7-8*

Clay or Playdough

2 c. flour
½ c. cornstarch
1 Tbsp. powdered alum

2 c. water
1 c. salt
1 Tbsp. oil

Place all ingredients in saucepan. Stir constantly over low heat until mixture thickens into dough consistency. Remove from heat and let cool until it can be handled. Place on foil or waxed paper or Formica top. Knead like bread until smooth. Add coloring, if desired. Store in airtight container or plastic bag. This recipe keeps for months and is safe and nontoxic.

—*Mrs. Amos Diener, Sullivan, IL*

Silly Putty

3 c. warm water, divided
2 c. Elmer's Glue®

1 Tbsp. borax

Mix 1½ c. warm water and glue together. Add remaining water and borax. Mix, using your hands. It will not seem to mix together, but keep pulling and playing with it until it falls together.

—*Mrs. Amos Diener, Sullivan, IL*

The true measure of a man is how he treats someone

whom he thinks can do him absolutely no good.

Add some cornstarch to hot vinegar water to wash windows. It will wipe easier and sparkle more. And is not as harsh as ammonia.

When adding raisins to granola, do so after toasting. This will prevent them from hardening.

If you feel keyed up at bedtime, ½ tsp. honey may help you relax.

Edible flowers: Did you ever think of washing the little flowers your children pick, and pushing them into the frosting of their birthday cake? Or they can serve as a simple, but pretty, decoration on a pudding or an unfrosted cake. They add a cheery touch and flavor when tossed into salads too. The blossoms in the following list are edible: bee balm, chive blossoms, daylily, geranium, hollyhock, impatiens, Johnny-jump-up, lavender, lilac, mint flower, pansy, rose, snapdragon, and violet (that grows in our yard and fields).

Instead of using Tenderquick to cure hams or bacon use: 2 gal. water, 2 c. salt, and ¼ c. vinegar (which works as a tenderizer). For large hams let cure for 7-10 days. Bacon only 5 days.

Can't have vinegar? Try lemon juice.

Fly spray for horses: 1 gal. white vinegar, 1 c. dish soap, 20 drops peppermint oil, 10 drops citronella oil. Mix in pump sprayer or small batch in a hand sprayer.

To remove the calcium buildup caused by hard water in teakettles: soak with pure white distilled vinegar until it rubs off easily. This also works for the water pails where water is kept in all the time.

Health Remedies & Hints

Fasting and Cleansing

Water fasting is one of the oldest health remedies known to man. If we abstain from all food, along with a *total physical and mental rest*, our bodies will automatically seek health through elimination of accumulated toxic sludge and poisons. Lengthy fasts can sometimes give near miraculous results, but should only be attempted under the care of an experienced health practitioner.

Juice cleansing is a more practical alternative for people with busy schedules. A good way to start is this 5-day cleanse.

> Day 1 – Eat only raw fruits and vegetables.
> Days 2-4 – Drink water, juices, herbal teas, and potassium broth (see health recipes in this cookbook).
> Day 5 – Eat only raw fruits and vegetables.
>
> Eat lightly for several more days to give your system time to adjust.

Too much fruit juice may cause a sugar imbalance if you are diabetic. Individual dietary needs may vary, depending on the state of health or toxicity.

A vegetarian diet can give great results when used during a cleansing period. Some people incorrectly conclude that this diet works all the time. People living a sedentary (or nonphysically active) lifestyle or in a southern climate may do all right for a while, but an active person, especially in the North, will probably need a steady supply of animal foods to give him strength and warmth through the long winters.

To eliminate chronic illnesses and greatly improve overall health, here are some ideas that will help. Get rid of parasites and candida, change your diet to all-natural, whole foods, and do a thorough cleanse of the liver, kidneys, and bowel. For stubborn cases these cleanses may need to be repeated quite often. Supplementing with digestive enzymes and beneficial bacteria, plus staying away from allergenic foods and drinks should all help the healing process.

Cough Syrup

1 pt. raw honey   1 medium onion
1 bulb garlic

Pour honey into a heavy saucepan. Take skins off all garlic cloves and slice garlics and onion into honey. Simmer for 20-30 minutes, stirring often. Strain, pour into glass jar, and use as needed. For bad coughs use 2 Tbsp. every 10 minutes or so.

—Mrs. Raymond Yutzy, Howe, IN

Cold Remedy

juice of ½ lemon   ¼-⅛ tsp. cayenne pepper
2 Tbsp. maple syrup or less   1 glass purified cold water

Mix all together. Drink first thing in the morning until your cold has disappeared.

—Mrs. Junior Detweiler, Redding, IA

Gall and Liver Treatment

½ c. cheese root   3 c. cold water
1 Tbsp. Cascara Sagrada

Place all ingredients in pan or glass teapot. Bring to boil and simmer till it's down to about 1 c. Strain and drink before going to bed. This must be taken on an empty stomach. Eat nothing for six hours before using the tea.

—Mrs. Allen A. Bontrager, LaGrange, IN

For a Stomachache

For a stomachache take as stock $^2/_3$ c. grated or shredded raw carrots. Add $^1/_3$ c. finely sliced, very ripe bananas and a few raisins or sliced dried figs. Celery or grated beets can also be used instead of carrots, although carrots work best. No nuts or cereals. Never mix nuts with wet fruits.

—*Mrs. John Detweiler, Marion, KY*

Super Antioxidant

2 medium carrots, chopped	1 oz. spinach
½ medium beet, chopped	4 sprigs fresh parsley
1 celery stalk with leaves, chopped	

Mix well and serve. Yield: 1 serving.

—*Mrs. Leroy B. Miller, Middlefield, OH*

Potassium Broth

Fill a large pot with 25% potato peelings, 25% carrot peelings and whole chopped beets, 25% chopped whole onions and garlic, and 25% whole chopped celery and dark greens. Add hot peppers to taste. Add enough water to just cover vegetables and simmer on very low heat for 2½ hours. Strain and drink only the broth. Use only organic vegetables.

Here is an interesting bit of information for us: In the early 1800s the average American ate less than 10 lb. of processed, refined sugars in one year. Today, two hundred years later, the average American eats over 150 lb. in the same amount of time.

Liver Flush

4 Tbsp. Epsom salts	½ c. olive oil
3 c. water	2 lemons or 1 grapefruit

Eat a no-fat breakfast and lunch. Don't eat or drink anything after 2:00. Mix together water and Epsom salts until dissolved. Pour into a jar and put in the refrigerator. At 6:00 and again at 8:00 drink ¾ c. Epsom salt water. A little before 10:00 squeeze the lemons or grapefruit and mix the juice with olive oil. Shake well in a pint jar.

Drink this at 10:00 and go straight for bed. Lie on your back. Sometime after 6:00 the next morning, take ¾ c. Epsom salt water and again 2 hours later. Two hours after your last dose of salts you may drink juice and later eat fruit. Eat lightly after that. By evening you should feel recovered.

Do this on a day like Saturday, so you can rest the next day. It is recommended that you do a parasite program first and also make sure your kidneys and bladder are working well.

Natural Pedialyte (for fever and vomiting)

2 c. warm water	¾ tsp. soda
2 Tbsp. honey	½ tsp. salt

Mix all together. Give as needed.
Note: Babies under a year old should not be given honey. Maple syrup may be substituted.

—*Mary Fisher, Rebersburg, PA*

I can evade questions without help; what I need is answers.
—*John F. Kennedy*

Homemade Tooth Powder

1 c. soda
¾ c. salt

½ tsp. oil of cloves or oil
of cinnamon or oil of
wintergreen

Blend soda and salt together and add oil of your choice. Keep in tightly covered container. To use, sprinkle on wet toothbrush and use instead of toothpaste. Actually whitens teeth and makes healthier gums. The oil part may be omitted or add even more depending on taste buds.

—Gertie Troyer, Loganville, WI

Herbal Scrub

½ c. oatmeal
¼ c. cornmeal

¼ c. dried lavender

Grind all ingredients in a blender and store in an airtight container. For a facial scrub, apply a small amount to damp skin, scrub gently, then rinse with warm water.

—Mrs. Leroy B. Miller, Middlefield, OH

Salve for Chest Colds

Melt 2 Tbsp. butter. Chop 3 large cloves garlic and 1 medium onion. Fry in butter, stirring often so it won't burn. Fry for 10 minutes or so. Strain and add 3 drops peppermint oil or eucalyptus oil. Let set until it hardens. Use for rubbing chest, back, and bottoms of feet.

—Mrs. Raymond Yutzy, Howe, IN

Herbal Salve

1 c. lard	1 doz. dried plantain leaves
1 goldenseal root or 1½ capsule	½ dozen dried comfrey leaves
small handful dried calendula flowers	2 Tbsp. beeswax, melted

Melt lard and steep herbs in it for half a day. Keep it hot, but not boiling. When done, strain through a thin cloth and squeeze rest of oil out of herbs. Now slowly stir beeswax into lard. Stir until well mixed. Pour into small containers. If it gets too hard add a little more lard. It will keep longer if you keep it in a cool place. The fresher the lard, the longer it'll last. Very healing for cuts, cold sores, scratches, chapped lips, etc.

—*Lydia Hostetler, Danville, OH*

Salve for Burns

1 gram alum ($^1/_5$ tsp.)	2 egg whites
1 c. lard	

Mix together alum and lard. Add egg whites and mix thoroughly. This is very effective for large burns. Spread on cloth and cover burn. It's also good for sunburns. Keep in small containers in the freezer to have ready when needed.

—*Mary Showalter, Mt. Solon, VA*

Solution for Cuts and Wounds

¼ c. cider vinegar	1 Tbsp. salt
1 Tbsp. soda	⅛ tsp. alum

Mix all ingredients and dissolve in a pint of water as hot as you can stand and soak wound 3 times a day.

—*Gertie Troyer, Loganville, WI*

For Croup

At the first sign of croup (dry, raspy cough), rub the feet with salve for chest colds. Then chop up garlic, put them in stockings, and put on the sick one's feet, making sure the garlic is spread right beneath the toes on the bottom of the feet. If you are afraid the garlic will blister the feet make a thin pouch of cotton material and put the garlic in there and then in the sock. You may have to put garlic on several times.

—*Mrs. Raymond Yutzy, Howe, IN*

For Earache

Using salve for chest colds, rub right in front of the ears and right behind the ears all the way down the neck. Use firm pressure but not too hard for the very young, and always rub down, not upwards. Also rub right beneath the jaw bone, starting right beneath the ear and working forward to the chin. Do this several times. This is also for sore throat.

—*Mrs. Raymond Yutzy, Howe, IN*

For Sore Throat

Take vinegar and make it strong with salt and red pepper and gargle often.

You are never fully dressed until you wear a smile.

To Soothe and Heal Cold Sores

8 ml. tea tree oil, 5 ml. lavender oil, 12 ml. sweet almond oil. Combine in a sterilized dropper bottle and shake well. Apply as needed.

For a Great Body Cleanser

Mix 2 Tbsp. freshly squeezed lemon juice with 2 Tbsp. maple syrup in a glass of water. Use daily as an energizer, a cleanser, and as a refreshing, nourishing drink.

For Coughs

Mixed with lemon juice, honey is an excellent remedy for simple coughs.

The Wisdom of Daily Life

Watch the sunrise at least once a year.

Plant flowers every spring.

Look people in the eye.

Compliment three people every day.

Live beneath your means.

Choose your life's mate carefully. From this one decision will come 90% of your happiness or misery.

Live so that when your children think of fairness, caring, and integrity, they think of you.

Don't postpone joy.

More Garden Tips

For moles and potato scab: After your garden is plowed throw several bags of lime onto it by handfuls. It will look white all over. Then disc it into the ground. The moles seemed to disappear the first year. I also have very little problem with scab on potatoes since putting on the lime.

To catch white butterflies that attack cabbage: Mix 1 c. sugar, 2 c. molasses, 1 c. vinegar, and 1 banana peel. Add ¾ gal. water. Fill an ice cream pail ¾ full and cut a hole 1" wide and 4"-5" long in the lid and set among the cabbage plants.

Spray for blight: 1 part buttermilk to 9 parts water. Spray every 10 days for blight.

In fall when tomato season is about over bring in one of your favorite tomatoes and slice. In a Cool Whip® container put approximately 3" soil. On top of that put one medium-thick slice of tomato. Put on lid and store in a cool dry place. On Valentine's Day or later bring out the container, add a thin layer of soil, and water it. Keep at room temperature and soon you'll have tomato sprouts.

Sources

Radiant Life
P.O. Box 765
Nicasio, CA 94946
888-593-8333

Celtic salt, coconut and olive oil, butter and cod liver oil

Really Raw Honey Company
3500 Boston St., Suite 32
Baltimore, MD 21224
800-732-5729

Honey

G. E. M. Cultures
30301 Sherwood Rd.,
Fort Brag, CA 95473
707-964-2922

Sourdough bread cultures

Lehman's
P.O. Box 41
Kidron, OH 44636
877-438-5346

Sorghum, maple syrup, kitchenware, grain mills

Wal-Mart Super Center

Schmucker's Natural Peanut Butter

Bio Supply, Ltd.
6-310 Goldstream Ave.
Victoria, British Columbia
Canada, V98 2W3

Yogurt, cheese, and kefir starters, kefir grains, grain mills

New England Cheesemaking Supply
292 Main St.
Ashfield, MA 01330

Yogurt, cheese, and kefir starters, rennet

Grain and Salt Supply
273 Fairway Dr.
Asheville, NC 28805
800-867-7258

Celtic sea salt, seasonings, whole grains

John and Elizabeth Drudge
RR#2, Wroxeter, Ontario
N0G 2X0
519-291-2819

Maple syrup

The Urban Homemaker
P. O. Box 72
Paonia, CO 81428
800-55-BREAD

Aternative Sweeteners, Real salt, herbs, whole wheat berries, water purifiers

If you need ingredients that are not listed by these sources, contact your local health food store.

Health Related Periodicals

Weston A. Price Foundation
PMB 106-380
4200 Wisconsin Ave NW
Washington, DC 20016
202-333-4325

Price-Pottenger Foundation
P. O. Box 2614
La Mesa, CA 91943
619-462-7600

Second Opinion Publishing
P. O. Box 467939
Atlanta, GA 31146
800-728-2288

Books

Nutrition and Physical Degeneration
by Weston A. Price

Nourishing Traditions
by Sally Fallon

Enzyme Nutrition
by Edward Howell

The Diet Cure
by Julia Ross

Tired – So Tired and the Yeast Connection
by William G. Crook

Unraveling the Mystery of Autism
by Karyn Seroussi

Restoring Your Digestive Health
by Jordan S. Rubin and Joseph Brasco

What the Bible Says About Healthy Living
by Rex Russel

Index